HARRY TRUMAN'S
INDEPENDENCE

THE CENTER OF THE WORLD

JON TAYLOR

Charleston  London

THE
History
PRESS

Published by The History Press
Charleston, SC 29403
www.historypress.net

Copyright © 2013 by Jon Taylor
All rights reserved

Cover images: Truman home (front) by Jeff Wade. All other images courtesy of the
Truman Library.

First published 2013

Manufactured in the United States

ISBN 978.1.60949.596.1

Library of Congress CIP data applied for.

To all who have been, are and will be Truman's neighbors…but especially for Liz.

Contents

Acknowledgements

H *arry Truman's Independence: The Center of the World* marks my fourth book on some aspect of Harry Truman's life and presidency. Harry Truman is an intensely interesting and yet contradictory person. On the surface, he looks uncomplicated, but digging beneath the surface of his life and the life of his community quickly reveals a complicated person and place. Understanding the complexities of one place does not come without help from those who have been a part of that place for a long time, and it also comes through sustained and methodical research, which I have conducted for almost twenty years.

In 1993, the National Park Service hired me on a term appointment to serve as historian at the Harry S Truman National Historic Site. The appointment was later converted to a permanent position, and as historian at the site, my supervisors Karen Tinnin and Carol Dage allowed me wide latitude to explore the vast holdings of the Truman Library to mine it for information that might help guide the park's interpretive, curatorial and management decisions. For a person who had just finished a master's degree in history, this was a dream come true, and it also opened the door between the National Park Service and the Harry S. Truman Library and Museum. I would like to thank Karen and Carol for giving me the leeway to conduct research while I was at the park from 1993 to 1998.

When I walked through the door of the Truman Library and Museum for the first time, I was met by an incredible array of Truman Library staff, who have become lifelong partners in the pursuit to understand not only who Harry Truman was but also his community. One of the first persons to greet me when I walked into the research room for the first time was Elizabeth Safly. Liz was from Independence, and she began work at the library in 1966. She possessed an incredible working knowledge of not only the library but also how Independence worked. She passed along much of that knowledge and collected some of it in her famous "Vertical File" that she maintained in the research room, and some of her insights have informed sections of this book. I was hoping that Liz might have been able to see this book; however, she passed away in September 2012. This book is dedicated to Liz Safly, who will always be the heart and soul of the research room of the Truman Library.

At the Truman Library, I also met one of the most able and helpful cadre of archivists ever assembled at a presidential library. At one point or another, I have benefitted from the expertise of Dr. Samuel Rushay, Dr. Randy Sowell, David Cark, Tammy Williams, Amy Williams, Dennis Bilger, Pauline Testerman, Jan Davis, Sharie Simon and Jim Armistead. Special Assistant to the Director Raymond Geselbracht has also been helpful, as have Curator Clay Bauske and Truman Library director Dr. Michael Devine.

Finally, thanks go to Truman's neighbors—and there are far too many to list here—who have worked a tireless number of hours preserving their own homes, and some have encouraged the city to preserve the Truman Heritage District and the Harry S Truman Historic District, National Historic Landmark. Notable neighbors, to name a few, include Patrick Steele, Wendy Shay, Brian and Sharon Snyder, Brent Schondelmeyer, Lee Williams and Sally Schwenk.

I have also valued the relationships that I have developed over the years with my colleagues throughout the National Park Service, especially Dr. William P. "Pat" O'Brien and Dr. Rachel Franklin-Weekley. Former superintendent of Harry S Truman NHS Jim Sanders and the City of Independence also advocated for the successful expansion of the Truman NHL in 2011.

Finally, my acknowledgements would not be complete without thanking Jeff Wade, park ranger at Harry S Truman National Historic Site. Jeff has a passion for understanding the importance of interpreting Harry Truman within the context of his neighborhood, and this book would not be complete without the maps that he developed to illustrate the various periods in Truman's life.

Introduction

On January 21, 1953, the train that carried Harry and Bess Truman arrived at the Truman Depot in Independence. Harry Truman stepped off that train in his hometown for the first time as an ex-president. His Secret Service detail was gone, and he was expected to quietly resume his place in the community. The train ride from Washington to Independence was probably one of the longest and perhaps most reflective trips the ex-president had ever taken. When he left office on that cold January day and passed the reins of government to Dwight Eisenhower, his approval rating hovered at about 30 percent. Those ratings were driven down by the Korean War, which had not ended, as well as some scandals that rocked his administration toward the end of his presidency. As the train approached the depot, he probably wondered whether he had let his hometown, state and nation down by the decisions he made as president. Simply put, in January 1953, Truman thought that his historical legacy hung in the balance, and he looked to his hometown as a place of refuge and strength from his political career, as he had since he was elected to the U.S. Senate in 1934. His hometown also offered him the opportunity to reflect back on his personal history. For the next eighteen years, he oversaw the creation or re-creation of his presidential legacy from the comfort of the community that he called "the Center of the World"—Independence, Missouri.

This book is about Harry Truman's Independence. He spent sixty-four years of his life in one community, and the experiences he had in Independence influenced his life; the fact that he became president of the United States also had an impact on Independence. The city was also home to his wife's family, and together with the Truman family, the Gates/Wallace families played important roles in the community's history. While Independence is often associated with Harry Truman, the city's landscape was also the setting for the settling of the West, as the Santa Fe, California and Oregon Trails all passed through the city during the first half and the beginning of the second half of the nineteenth century. The trails' history, while nationally significant, is joined by another equally important historical legacy: the city's religious history. In 1831, Joseph Smith, founder of the Church of Jesus Christ of Latter-Day Saints, proclaimed the city "Zion," and his followers flocked to the "Center Place" to build it up in anticipation of Christ's return. Unfortunately, the Saints, as Smith's followers were called, were forcefully removed from the city in 1833, only to return in the late nineteenth and early twentieth centuries as the Reorganized Church of Jesus Christ of Latter-Day Saints (RLDS) and the Church of Jesus Christ of Latter-Day Saints (LDS). Today, the RLDS church is known as the Community of Christ.

Truman was a product of this complicated landscape, yet no study has attempted to fully explain how he interacted with this landscape, particularly after he became president. While it would be incorrect to assume that the community completely embraced his politics, it did relish the fact that one of its own served as president of the United States. The fact that Truman was president focused intense scrutiny on the city, especially when he returned for visits, during the holidays or when he returned to vote in his home precinct. In November 1948, Independence took center stage in the close presidential election. When Truman returned home for these visits, he liked to pop out of his residence at 219 North Delaware and take a stroll through his neighborhood and town square. These walks pleased those he encountered along the way and gave him the opportunity to connect or reconnect with the people in his community. He was one of the few twentieth-century presidents to utilize walks as a way to connect with the people—his constituents, or "customers" as he called them.

Truman was the president who presided over the end of World War II and the beginning of the Cold War, and he relished the opportunity to continue to interact with his neighbors while he was president. During the Cold War, he talked about what it meant to be a good neighbor. The neighborliness that he enjoyed in Independence was something that he wanted the world to embrace during the Cold War.

Harry S Truman Historic District National Historic Landmark

Independence, Missouri

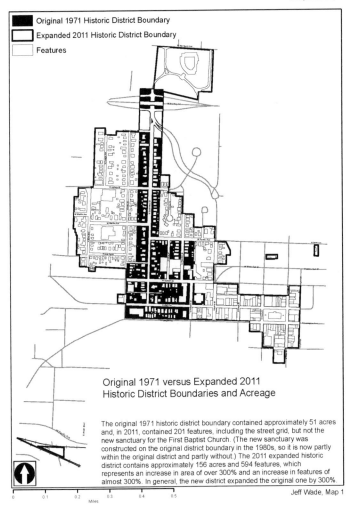

Original 1971 Historic District Boundary

Expanded 2011 Historic District Boundary

Features

Original 1971 versus Expanded 2011
Historic District Boundaries and Acreage

The original 1971 historic district boundary contained approximately 51 acres and, in 2011, contained 201 features, including the street grid, but not the new sanctuary for the First Baptist Church. (The new sanctuary was constructed on the original district boundary in the 1980s, so it is now partly within the original district and partly without.) The 2011 expanded historic district contains approximately 156 acres and 594 features, which represents an increase in area of over 300% and an increase in features of almost 300%. In general, the new district expanded the original one by 300%.

Jeff Wade, Map 1

Map by Jeff Wade.

Through those walks, he continued to please Independence residents and people who gathered outside the fence at 219 North Delaware after he left office in 1953. He also established his presidential library, occasionally spoke out on national and international issues and wrote books that described his impact on history. He also used this time to reconnect with his family.

Harry S Truman Historic District National Historic Landmark

Independence, Missouri

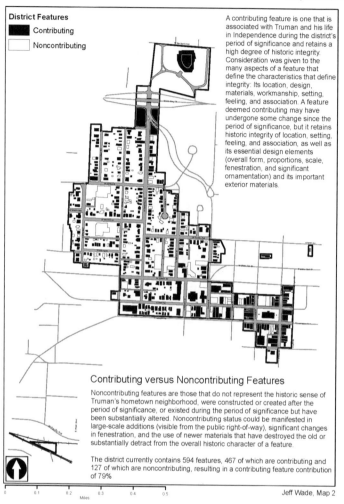

District Features

▪ Contributing

☐ Noncontributing

A contributing feature is one that is associated with Truman and his life in Independence during the district's period of significance and retains a high degree of historic integrity. Consideration was given to the many aspects of a feature that define the characteristics that define integrity: Its location, design, materials, workmanship, setting, feeling, and association. A feature deemed contributing may have undergone some change since the period of significance, but it retains historic integrity of location, setting, feeling, and association, as well as its essential design elements (overall form, proportions, scale, fenestration, and significant ornamentation) and its important exterior materials.

Contributing versus Noncontributing Features

Noncontributing features are those that do not represent the historic sense of Truman's hometown neighborhood, were constructed or created after the period of significance, or existed during the period of significance but have been substantially altered. Noncontributing status could be manifested in large-scale additions (visible from the public right-of-way), significant changes in fenestration, and the use of newer materials that have destroyed the old or substantially detract from the overall historic character of a feature.

The district currently contains 594 features, 467 of which are contributing and 127 of which are noncontributing, resulting in a contributing feature contribution of 79%

0   0.1   0.2   0.3   0.4   0.5
Miles

Jeff Wade, Map 2

Map by Jeff Wade.

His cousins, Nellie and Ethel Noland, lived right across the street, and two brothers-in-law lived right behind the house that Truman shared with Bess, and he enjoyed visiting with them, as well as forging new relationships with his grandchildren who visited from New York.

Harry S Truman Historic District National Historic Landmark
Independence, Missouri

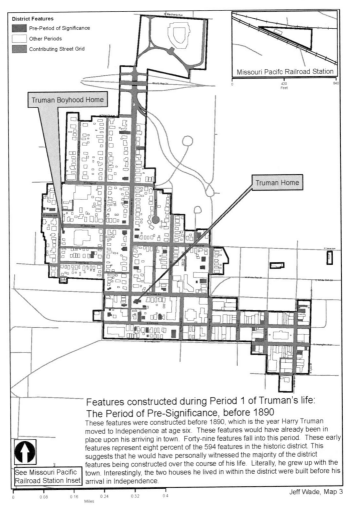

District Features
- Pre-Period of Significance
- Other Periods
- Contributing Street Grid

Missouri Pacifc Railroad Station

Truman Boyhood Home

Truman Home

Features constructed during Period 1 of Truman's life:
The Period of Pre-Significance, before 1890
These features were constructed before 1890, which is the year Harry Truman moved to Independence at age six. These features would have already been in place upon his arriving in town. Forty-nine features fall into this period. These early features represent eight percent of the 594 features in the historic district. This suggests that he would have personally witnessed the majority of the district features being constructed over the course of his life. Literally, he grew up with the town. Interestingly, the two houses he lived in within the district were built before his arrival in Independence.

See Missouri Pacific Railroad Station Inset

Jeff Wade, Map 3

Map by Jeff Wade.

Shortly before Harry Truman died on December 26, 1972, he agreed to allow the secretary of the interior to establish the Harry S Truman Historic District, National Historic Landmark (Truman NHL) to honor his sixty-four-year association with his neighborhood. At the time of the designation,

13

Harry S Truman Historic District National Historic Landmark

Independence, Missouri

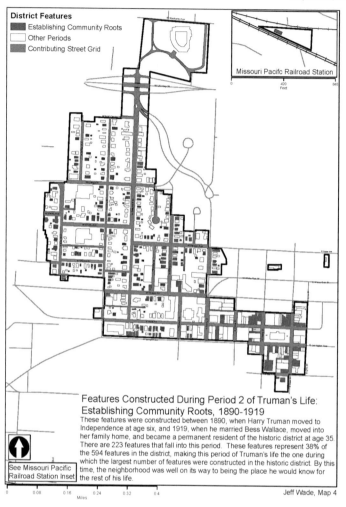

District Features
- Establishing Community Roots
- Other Periods
- Contributing Street Grid

Missouri Pacifc Railroad Station

Features Constructed During Period 2 of Truman's Life:
Establishing Community Roots, 1890-1919
These features were constructed between 1890, when Harry Truman moved to Independence at age six, and 1919, when he married Bess Wallace, moved into her family home, and became a permanent resident of the historic district at age 35. There are 223 features that fall into this period. These features represent 38% of the 594 features in the district, making this period of Truman's life the one during which the largest number of features were constructed in the historic district. By this time, the neighborhood was well on its way to being the place he would know for the rest of his life.

See Missouri Pacific Railroad Station Inset

Jeff Wade, Map 4

Map by Jeff Wade.

the Truman NHL was composed primarily of residential homes; however, in 2011, the secretary of the interior approved an expansion of the 1971 designation, which included many structures on the Independence Square, including the Independence Courthouse.

The Gates/Wallace and Truman Families Come to Independence, 1865-1902

The schoolteacher, my friends, is the most important asset, next to the mother of a child, that he has. The teachers of children in the lower grades—the primary grades—makes a greater impression on the children of the country than any other person with whom he comes in contact. And I speak from experience. I can still remember my first and second and fourth and fifth grade teacher—who made a tremendous impression on me—got me started in the right direction. And I will have to admit that I may not have ended up as I thought I should. But then they were not to blame for that.[1]
—Harry Truman, Jefferson City, Missouri, October 8, 1952

Independence, Missouri, was a frontier community when the town was formally organized in 1827 as the county seat of Jackson County. The community became an important stop and outfitting center on the Santa Fe, California and Oregon Trails from the 1820s to 1860. The trails' trade attracted a diverse lot of individuals, and it was not uncommon if one traversed the Independence Square that you could find Anglos, Hispanics, Native Americans, free blacks and enslaved blacks walking the streets and entering into partnerships that had international connections.[2] The Civil War reorganized the town, as it did most towns in Missouri after the war, and its residents continued to redefine the town from 1860 to 1900. Harry S. Truman and Bess Wallace Truman's family roots were firmly planted in Independence. Bess's family had a stronger connection to the town, as her maternal and paternal great-grandfathers had come to Independence

before 1890, the year when Harry Truman's family came. However, unlike Truman's forebears, who were thoroughly southern, Bess's forebears were both northern and southern.

George W. Gates and his wife, Sarah, might have arrived in Independence from Illinois as early as March 1865, shortly before the Civil War came to a close in April. In September, he wrote to his oldest son, George P. Gates, who was living in Port Byron, Illinois, and described the city as "full of professional operators, lawyers and preachers...who will be glad to leave after they find out that those who have been rebels are not afraid to return, assert their rights & live here." He continued his assessment of Independence by calling it the "most desirable place to live." It is not entirely clear why George W. Gates was drawn to Independence; however, he quickly settled in the town, and in March 1866, he informed his son that he purchased twenty-three acres for $3,000 on the east side of the city. His acreage included orchards and pastureland.[3]

George W. and Sarah Gates joined the First Presbyterian Church in January 1866, and

Top: George W. Gates. *Truman Library.*

Left: Sarah D. Gates. *Truman Library.*

Independence home of George W. and Sarah Gates. *Truman Library.*

he held various positions in the church including deacon, elder and choir director. By 1867, he was appointed to a one-year term on the Jackson County Court, and from 1871 to 1872, he represented Jackson County in the Missouri legislature. When he finished his term, he returned to Independence, where he served several terms on the county court. George W. Gates died on July 5, 1890, from injuries he sustained when he fell off of a horse that bolted after it was spooked by fireworks. Sarah Gates died on August 19, 1889.

On September 2, 1866, George P. Gates informed his father by letter that he was planning to relocate his family to Independence. George Porterfield Gates was born on April 2, 1835, in Lunenbergh, Vermont. He moved to Rock Island County, Illinois, in about 1853, and in 1860, he married Elizabeth Emery in Port Byron, Illinois. Evidence suggests that the family arrived in Independence in November 1866, which meant that Madge Gates, the couple's oldest daughter, who was born on August 4, 1862, was three years old when she came to Independence. She was joined by younger sisters Maud, who was born in 1864, and Myra, who was born in 1866.[4]

In Port Byron, Gates served as secretary of the Port Byron Oil and Mineral Land Company and was a partner in Gates Moore & Company, which was a retail dealer in Port Byron. He was also active in the Masonic organization, where he was a member of Philo Lodge No. 436. It is not entirely clear what finally enticed George P. Gates to come to Independence,

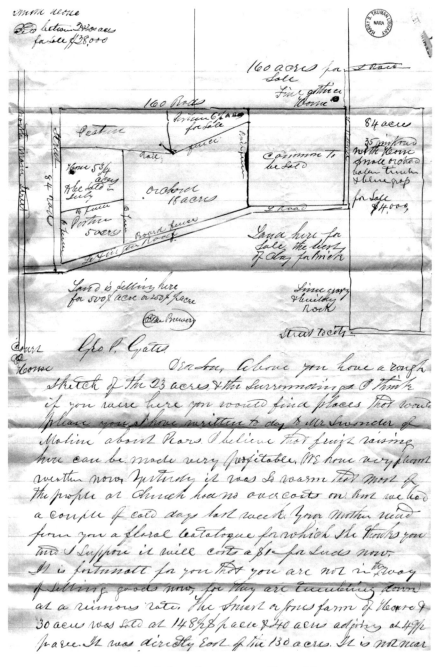

George W. Gates's sketch of his Independence property. *Truman Library.*

although it was clear that his father's relocation to the city in 1865 was an important factor. He probably came seeking to apply his business skills to new opportunities that presented themselves in a frontier town that was seeking to rebuild itself after the Civil War and once again resume its place as an outfitting center for those traveling into the West.

Fittingly, Gates participated in America's westward expansion during this period because he became involved with a sawmill operation in Independence that was responsible for providing

George Porterfield Gates, Bess Truman's maternal grandfather. *Truman Library.*

lumber used in the construction of the Hannibal Bridge in Kansas City. The construction of the bridge was completed in 1869 and was significant because it was the first railroad bridge that crossed the Missouri River at Kansas City. Ultimately, the construction of the Hannibal Bridge across the Missouri River at Kansas City resulted in the displacement of St. Joseph as an important outfitting city for those traveling into the West. Gates partnered with A.F. Anderson in the firm of Gates and Anderson, which was headquartered at the northwest corner of Maple and Liberty Streets.[5] In 1872, Gates organized the Jackson County and Osage Valley Mining and Smelting Company. In 1876, he formed a partnership with William H. Waggoner—whose father, Peter Waggoner, had come to Independence from Philadelphia after the war—and established a flour mill. Gates traveled across the South in the 1880s and marketed Queen of the Pantry Flour, which was the brand the company became noted for. Gates served as the secretary-treasurer for the organization, and the business was incorporated as the Waggoner-Gates Milling Company. He continued his interest in the milling company until his death, but he also maintained other business pursuits.[6]

In the 1890s, George P. Gates was involved with the J.F. Crawford Lumber Company and also served as president of the American Lumber Company. He was very active in the financial affairs of his community and

The brothers of George Porterfield Gates. *Left to right, standing*: Walter and Edward. *Left to right, sitting*: Frederick, Charles and George. *Truman Library.*

was frequently asked to support numerous community efforts, including the creation of the Kansas City Ladies College, which was affiliated with the Presbyterian Church. The printed materials for the college in 1884 listed his occupation as a "Capitalist." It was a fitting description for someone whose business interests were not just limited to one business venture. He came to Independence after the war, looking for new business opportunities, and he invested in them if he thought he could realize a profit.[7]

It is not exactly certain where George P. Gates, his wife and daughters lived after they arrived in Independence in 1866, although evidence

This page: Waggoner-Gates Mill. *Truman Library.*

suggests that they stayed with his father and mother. In June 1867, George P. Gates purchased lots two and three in James F. Moore's Addition, which were located along North Delaware Street. Judging from the purchase price of $700, historians believe that there was some structure located on

Elizabeth Emery Gates, Bess Truman's maternal grandmother. *Truman Library.*

Maud, Madge and Myra Gates, 1872. *Truman Library.*

the lots when Gates purchased them, and the family probably moved into this home. The family expanded in size after they moved in to include G. Walter Gates, who was born in 1868, and Frank E. Gates, who was born in 1871. In November 1868, Gates purchased two additional lots that he used as a garden and grazing area.[8]

By 1885, George P. Gates had distinguished himself as a capitalist, and he remodeled his existing home to reflect that wealth. At the time of the remodel, Madge Wallace, his daughter, had already married and had moved out of the home but was nearby in her own home at 117 West Ruby Street. Only his youngest child, fourteen-year-old Frank, remained at home. Gates secured the services of James W. Adams to oversee the complete renovation of the home. According to historian Ron Cockrell, Adams built "a two and one-half story mansion fronting on North Delaware." The *Independence Sentinel* noted that the Victorian home included "fourteen rooms, water and gas" systems, and at the time, the home was the most expensive residence in the city, valued at $8,000. Cockrell noted that the "1885 addition was built onto the west and north ends of the 1867

Number 219 North Delaware, the home that George Porterfield and Elizabeth Emery Gates remodeled in 1885. *Truman Library.*

structure." It is this remodeled residence that Harry and Bess Truman called home after they married in 1919, and they would continue to call 219 North Delaware home until their respective deaths in 1972 and 1982.

The marriage of Madge Gates to David W. Wallace on the evening of June 13, 1883, at the First Presbyterian Church represented a blending of the North and South that occurred in the community in the twenty years after the Civil War. David W. Wallace was born on June 15, 1860, in Independence to Benjamin F. and Virginia Willock Wallace. In contrast to George P. and George W. Gates, Benjamin F. Wallace was one of the first settlers to come to Jackson County in 1833. After the war, in 1869, he was elected as mayor of Independence, and like George W. Gates, Benjamin Wallace was also elected to the Missouri legislature and represented Jackson County at the time of his death in 1877, just a few years after George W. Gates had held the same position.

In spite of the northern roots of the Gates family, they did not seem to rub off on Madge Gates. In fact, one oral history interviewee described Madge as "symbolic of the old Southern ladies that I have been drilled in all my life. She was the nicest—she had the kind of Southern brogue. In my word she was a

Madge Gates, Bess's mother, 1881. *Truman Library.*

David W. Wallace, Bess's father, in Knights Templar attire. *Truman Library.*

typical Southern lady—just as kind and spoke in kind of a soft voice."[9] Apparently, the southerness of Independence had worn off.

Madge Gates Wallace and David W. Wallace settled in their new home on West Ruby, where Elizabeth "Bess" (or "Bessie") was born on February 13, 1885. David Wallace worked as the deputy recorder for the county; however, his paycheck was not enough to support his family, which also included Frank Gates Wallace, who was born to the couple on March 4, 1887. David sold his property on West Ruby and moved his family into the Gates house at 219 North Delaware. The move had to have been a blow to David Wallace. The family remained at 219 North Delaware until 1890, when they moved to a home farther north on Delaware.[10]

Shortly after the family's arrival at their new home at 608 North Delaware, Bess and Frank were greeted with a new addition to the family: a younger brother, George Porterfield Wallace, was born on May 1, 1892. Included with the new house were five outbuildings: a carriage house, a stable, a washhouse, a woodhouse and a privy. A large burr oak tree prominently marked the front yard; Bess and her brothers liked to climb it. Mary Paxton Keeley, who lived next door to the Wallaces at 614 North Delaware, became one of Bess's best friends. Keeley described the neighborhood in this manner:

The block had about twenty-seven children in it. Summer nights we had a curfew at nine and we played all these games. I remember my father had two cows and a horse—but he rented a barn down the street…We had a garden; my father bought the lot back of us and made it into a flower garden—the most beautiful flower garden in town. Of course, we had to have vegetables at first and we had all kinds of fruit trees.[11]

Keeley also noted that almost "everybody had a cook" and that most of the cooks were African American; however, she remembered that her

The Wallace family home at 608 North Delaware. *Truman Library.*

mother at one point hired two Swedish cooks, "but they were so brash that she [her mother] went back to the Negroes." She continued: "A cook didn't cost much money. Those cooks had a custom of taking all the leftovers home. They went home after the midday meal, and came back to get the supper. They always worked on Sunday because we had a better dinner. But they took home the remains…But I don't remember the Wallace cook or cooks."[12]

Keeley also recalled a community that was sharply divided socially by religion and described it as a "snobbish little town" where the Presbyterians "were top on the pole, then the Campbellites (The Christian Church); and then I guess, the North Methodists, and the Southern Methodists; the Baptists came about next; the Lutherans were the German part of the population; and there was a big Catholic Church, but most of its congregation was from out in the country." She described the "status of Mormons" as "just a cut above the Negro. People went to hear them sing in the Stone Church, but that was all. In business they did well, and my father had Mormon clients that he highly respected."[13]

Bess grew up in the home at 608 North Delaware. Mary Paxton Keeley remembered attending dances with Bess and playing card games during her adolescent years. She also remembered that "Bess always had more stylish hats than the rest of us did, or she wore them with more style."[14]

While Bess's social standing in the community dictated that she attend dances and dress appropriately for those occasions, she also participated in athletics. Keeley noted that "[Bess] was a fine athlete," that she was a "crack tennis player" and that she served as the "basket thrower" on the women's basketball team.[15]

Madge and David Wallace had two more daughters, born in the 1890s; however, they both died. One daughter, Madeline, died when she was three years old. The second daughter, born in early May 1898, lived only one day. The last child, David Frederick, known as "Fred," was born on January 7, 1900.[16]

In 1890, Independence was a bustling center of trade for the eastern or rural part of Jackson County, Missouri, when the Truman family arrived. In that year, the U.S. Census recorded 6,974 residents.[17] The heart and soul of the business community was the Independence Square, which flourished with banks, dry good stores and a few saloons, located on the south side of the square. On the outskirts of the business district sat an industrial area that featured the Queen of the Pantry flour mill. On the northwest boundary of the town stood Sugar Creek, focal point for a Standard Oil Refinery that opened after the turn of the twentieth century.

Left to right: Frank, unidentified girl, Fred, Bess and George Wallace. *Truman Library.*

According to Mary Ethel Noland, Harry Truman's first cousin, John A. Truman, and John's wife, Martha Ellen Truman, moved their young family to Independence in 1890 so they could take advantage of the public schools and because Independence was southern. Mary Ethel Noland remembered, "Independence was the center of learning in Jackson County. There were two colleges here at the time—girls' colleges—Woodland College at Waldo and Union Streets and Presbyterian College." She continued, noting, "Independence was still the place to go if you wanted to find culture and Kansas City was a kind of a Yankee Town, you know, and we were still a little sore about what the Yankees had done to us. So Yankee was kind of a bad word." She then noted, "Independence was Southern and Kansas City was not."[18]

John A. Truman was born on December 5, 1851, in Jackson County, Missouri, to Anderson Shipp Truman and Mary Jane (Holmes) Truman. John Truman's parents moved to Missouri in the fall of 1846 from Shelby County, Kentucky. Martha Ellen Truman's parents, Solomon and Harriet Young, also hailed from Shelby County and arrived in Missouri in 1841. Solomon Young had been a freighter along the trails and owned a large farm near Grandview, Missouri. John A. Truman married Martha Ellen Young

Wedding photo of John A. and Martha Ellen Truman, Harry Truman's parents, 1881. *Truman Library.*

on December 28, 1881, and for the next several years, the couple lived on several different Missouri farms.

When the couple arrived in Independence in December 1890, they had three young children in tow. Their oldest, Harry, was born on May 8, 1884, in Lamar, Missouri, about ninety miles south of Kansas City. Vivian Truman, Harry Truman's younger brother, was born on a farm in Cass County on April 25, 1886. The last child, Mary Jane, was born on August 12, 1889, at the Young farm in Grandview.[19]

The family moved into a house on South Crysler Avenue that had a few acres of land to accommodate John Truman's continued interest in livestock trading. According to his son, when the family arrived, his father operated a farm located southeast of town that served as his base of buying and selling cattle, hogs and sheep; however, the home place on Crysler featured a few barns, a chicken yard, a strawberry bed and a fine garden. Harry recalled, "We always had ponies and horses to ride, goats to hitch to our little wagon, which was made like a big one."[20] Ethel Noland remembered the yellow tomatoes that her uncle, John Truman, grew in his garden. Ethel also recalled that John Truman called it a "peach tomato," and she described it as "beautiful," with a "fine flavored" taste.[21] Harry also remembered that his parents began taking him and his two younger siblings to Sunday school at the First Presbyterian Church located at Lexington and Pleasant Streets, where he also met Bess Wallace for the first time.[22]

From 1890 to 1896, the Truman family lived at the Crysler Avenue house. In 1896, John Truman moved his family to 909 West Waldo, which put the family on the outskirts of the neighborhood that the Gates and Wallace families called home. A neighbor, Henry Chiles, remembered that John A. Truman continued his livestock business when the family moved to Waldo:

> *Everybody in those days had a few cows and—a little bit farther out this is big stock country—he would buy cattle, one cow or two cows. One time in particular I remember, he came in with a calf across his saddle and the old mother cow following up. He didn't have to tie her, she just followed the calf. He had bought the cow and calf and come in. And he had a lot on the corner of Waldo that run back to the alley. Oh, it covered several lots wide and had a barn and he kept one to a dozen cattle in there all the time. He'd slick them up and if necessary he'd drive them to Kansas City and sell them to the stockyard. In those days we didn't have any trucks, of course, and the only way to get them there was to ship them on the train or drive them. So people within fifty miles of the stockyard didn't ever do anything but drive them right on down Fifth Street right into the stockyard.*[23]

Harry described his new neighborhood as "most pleasant" because there were plenty of children for him to play with, including Henry Chiles and his brother, Morton, who were the same age as Harry and Vivian. However, Henry and Morton were not the only friends Harry made on West Waldo. There were others, and Harry remembered them well, as they made up what came to be known as the West Waldo Gang:

> *Next door, to the east, lived the Burrus family. There were three boys and five girls, three of the girls the ages of Vivian, Mary, and me. Next door east of the Burrus family lived the Wrights…Arthur Wright was the oldest boy and was a partner with his father in a tailor shop in Kansas City. Lofton Wright was the second boy in the family…The youngest boy was named James, who became a very good friend of mine and who died of a heart attack at the age of thirty-five.*
>
> *West on Waldo lived the Pittman family…and Bernard, who was Vivian's age and his pal. South and west of us on Blue Avenue [now Truman Road] lived the Smith boys, and at the other end of the block, just back of us on White Oak Street, lived the Chiles family with two boys, Henry and Morton…At the Corner of Delaware and Waldo, east of us, were the Sawyers, the Wallaces, and the Thomases. Lock Sawyer was older than we were, and the Wallaces were a year or two younger. Bess, Frank, and George Wallace all belonged to the Waldo Avenue gang. Across the street at Woodland College were Paul and*

Helen Bryant. Paul and Vivian were great friends and raised pigeons and game chickens in partnership.[24]

Chiles remembered the Waldo Avenue Gang outings:

We not only played cowboys, we really were cowboys. The Trumans, as I say, came off the farm and my father came off the farm, and we both had horses. Each one of us boys had a pony and we'd play real cowboys, and I am not fooling. We would rope each other and drag around. I remember one incident. When we'd practice we would ride down the alley as fast as we could and see if we could lariat a post, a fence post, and then if we caught it we would turn the rope loose and come on back. One time, some way or the other my rope got caught around the saddle horn and when I roped the post, come to the end of the rope, there we both were, me and the saddle, and the horse went on. But I remember Harry used to come down there, but [he] didn't—I don't remember ever seeing him on a horse.[25]

Chiles also noticed that Harry did not always participate in all of the physical pursuits in which his fellow Waldo Street Gang members engaged. Chiles remembered that Harry "took an almost daily music lesson and he came by with a great big leather music folio or portfolio, or whatever you call it, under his arm. He would come by and watch us and maybe he would hit a lick or two in the shinny or try to throw a rope." Chiles continued:

They wanted to call him sissy, but they just didn't do it because they had a lot of respect for him. I remember one time we were playing, I think, another game that we played, Jesse James or robbers, and we were the Dalton brothers out in Kansas—that's about the time they got killed—and we were arguing about them. Harry came in—we got the history mixed up ourselves—but Harry came in and straightened it out, just who were the Dalton brothers and how many got killed. Things like that the boys had a lot of respect for; they didn't call him sissy. Nowadays they probably would.[26]

One of the reasons why the Truman family came to Independence was to attend the town's well-respected public schools. When Harry lived in the house on Crysler, he entered first grade in 1892 at the age of eight and attended the Noland School, located at 527 South Liberty Street, since it was the closest to his family's home on Crysler Avenue. Raymond Geselbracht

INDEPENDENCE PUBLIC SCHOOLS.

Term Reports of M _Harry Truman_

Columbian School. _A_ Class. _Second_ Grade.

189.4	SCHOLARSHIP.											ATTENDANCE.			ABS'NCE		TARDY.			
MONTHS AND TERMS.	SPELLING.	READING.	WRITING.	GEOGRAPHY.	U. S. HIST.	LANGUAGE.	GRAMMAR.	NUMBERS.	MENT. AR.	WRIT. AR.	HYGIENE.	DAYS PRES.	DAYS ABS.	TIMES T'DY.	DEPORTM'T.	Excused.	Unexcused.	Excused.	Unexcused.	SIGNATURE OF PARENT OR GUARDIAN.
FIRST TERM																				
SECOND TERM																				
THIRD TERM																				
YEARLY.																				

The parent or guardian is respectfully asked to examine carefully the Report, to sign it and send it back by the pupil,

Marion Dunne Teacher.

Harry Truman's second-grade report card. *Truman Library.*

noted that Truman's first-grade year began on September 13; however, his grade report noted that he did not attend until October 17.[27] In 1894, Harry contracted diphtheria, which left his legs, arms and throat paralyzed, and he had to drop out of school. Fortunately, he was able to recover, and he had to attend summer school at a new school: the Columbian school, which was located at 320 South River Boulevard, where he was able to catch up.

When Truman's family moved to West Waldo, he transferred for the fifth grade to the Ott School, which was located at the southwest corner of Liberty Street and College Avenue. Geselbracht noted that Truman "went back to [the] Columbian School for at least part of seventh grade, and back to Ott School again for his first year of high school." He split time between the Columbian School and the new Independence High School, located on the northwest corner of Pleasant and Maple Streets, for his second year of high school and spent his third and final year of high school at Independence High School.[28]

Harry reflected on the importance of the education he received in Independence and throughout the remainder of his life he maintained relationships with his former teachers during his political career long after he had left their classrooms. It seemed that the courses he took exposed him to places outside of Independence; Jackson County, Missouri; the United States; and the world, and their teaching ignited within him a passion for lifelong learning. Mize Peters was a fellow classmate of Harry Truman's in first grade, and he remembered, "He and I were seatmates in the first grade. In those days two children sat together in an old bench with a dividing board that ran down the center. Possibly six or eight benches were fastened together with a child on either side of each bench. Miss Myra Ewing was our teacher whom we loved very much."[29]

In his memoirs, Harry fondly remembered his first-grade teacher, Miss Mira Ewin, who he said "became a favorite" of his. Miss Minnie Ward was his second-grade teacher at the Noland School, and his summer school teacher at the Columbian School was Miss Jennie Clements. Truman skipped the third grade because of his excellent performance in summer school, and Miss Mamie Dunne taught him in fourth grade. History teacher Miss Maggie Phelps and English teacher Miss Tillie Brown taught Harry Truman in high school. Truman remembered that Brown was a "genius at making us appreciate good literature" and "made us want to read it." W.L.C. Palmer taught him science and later became the superintendent of Independence Public Schools. Palmer later married Ardelia Hardin, who taught Truman mathematics and Latin at the Independence high school. Of all of his teachers, Harry remarked, "I do not remember a bad teacher in all my experience. They were all different, of course, but they were the salt of the earth. They gave us our high ideals, and they hardly ever received more than forty dollars a month for it." Above the main entrance to the high school, W.L.C. Palmer placed the Latin phrase *Juventus Spes Mundi*, which meant, "Youth Hope of the World."[30]

In August 1900, the Noland family, including Harry's beloved cousins, Nellie and Ethel, moved to 216 North Delaware, which was conveniently located across the street from the Gates home at 219 North Delaware. The Noland family arrived in Independence in 1883. Ella Truman was the older sister of John A. Truman, Harry's father, and she married Joseph Tilford Noland on December 18, 1870. The couple had four

Harry S. Truman at age thirteen, 1897.
Truman Library.

children; however, their firstborn, an infant son, only lived three days. Ruth Truman Noland, the couple's first daughter, was born on August 3, 1876, followed by Ellen Tilford "Nellie" Noland on July 16, 1881, and Mary Ethel Noland on October 23, 1883.[31]

The Noland home was conveniently located on the route that both Bess (who was still living at 608 North Delaware) and Harry (who was

The Noland family home at 216 North Delaware. *Truman Library.*

Ethel Noland (on the left) with her sister, Nellie, in the front yard of 216 North Delaware, with 219 North Delaware in the background. *Truman Library.*

still living on West Waldo) would have to pass by on their way to high school. Harry and Bess studied together at the Noland house, and Nellie Noland, who was good in Latin, helped them both with their schoolwork. However, Ethel Noland remarked, "I don't know whether they got much Latin read or not because there was a lot of fun going on, and Harry had become interested in fencing. He had two foils, or rapiers…and so we would sometimes practice fencing, which we knew absolutely nothing about, but it was fun to try, and we had a porch and we had room here to play and have fun, generally, which we did, with a little Latin intermingled, maybe."[32]

On May 30, 1901, the students of the Independence High School class of 1901 gathered together one last time for graduation. Charlie Ross, whom Truman later tapped to be his press secretary, was selected as the top student in the class. The class gathered for a formal class portrait in front of the main entrance to the school.

The time Harry Truman spent in Independence from 1890 to 1902 was very important. What is interesting is that much like Bess's family, the Truman family moved around in the small town when he was a child. Harry's family moved

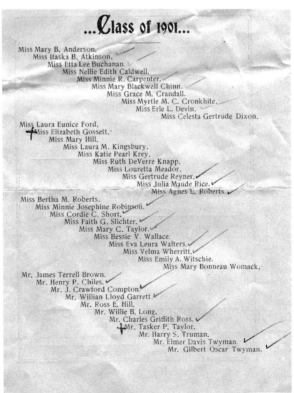

Above: Independence High School graduating class of 1901. Harry Truman is located on the back row, fourth person from the left. Bess Wallace is in the second row, first person from the right. Charlie Ross, who became Harry Truman's press secretary, is in the front row, first person from the left. Notice the Latin inscription *Juventus Spes Mundi* ("Youth Hope of the World") in the stained glass above the entrance to the school. *Truman Library.*

Right: Independence High School graduating class of 1901 graduation program. *Truman Library.*

...Class of 1901...

Miss Mary B. Anderson.
Miss Itaska B. Atkinson.
Miss Etta Lee Buchanan.
Miss Nellie Edith Caldwell.
Miss Minnie R. Carpenter.
Miss Mary Blackwell Chinn.
Miss Grace M. Crandall.
Miss Myrtle M. C. Cronkhite.
Miss Erle L. Devin.
Miss Celesta Gertrude Dixon.
Miss Laura Eunice Ford.
Miss Elizabeth Gossett.
Miss Mary Hill.
Miss Laura M. Kingsbury.
Miss Katie Pearl Krey.
Miss Ruth DeVerre Knapp.
Miss Louretta Meador.
Miss Gertrude Reyner.
Miss Julia Maude Rice.
Miss Agnes L. Roberts.
Miss Bertha M. Roberts.
Miss Minnie Josephine Robinson.
Miss Cordie C. Short.
Miss Faith G. Slichter.
Miss Mary C. Taylor.
Miss Bessie V. Wallace.
Miss Eva Leura Walters.
Miss Velma Wherritt.
Miss Emily A. Witschie.
Miss Mary Bonneau Womack.
Mr. James Terrell Brown.
Mr. Henry P. Chiles.
Mr. J. Crawford Compton.
Mr. Willian Lloyd Garrett.
Mr. Ross E. Hill.
Mr. Willie B. Long.
Mr. Charles Griffith Ross.
Mr. Tasker P. Taylor.
Mr. Harry S. Truman.
Mr. Elmer Davis Twyman.
Mr. Gilbert Oscar Twyman.

35

Harry S Truman Historic District National Historic Landmark

Independence, Missouri

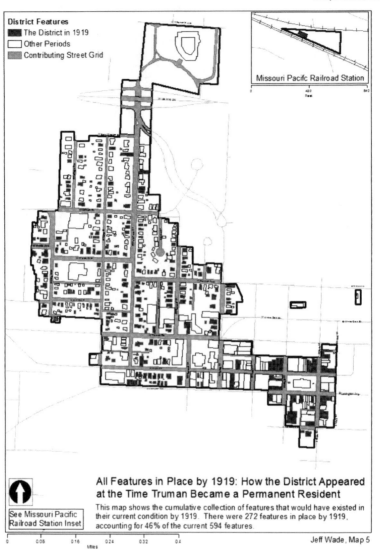

District Features
- The District in 1919
- Other Periods
- Contributing Street Grid

Missouri Pacifc Railroad Station

All Features in Place by 1919: How the District Appeared at the Time Truman Became a Permanent Resident

This map shows the cumulative collection of features that would have existed in their current condition by 1919. There were 272 features in place by 1919, accounting for 46% of the current 594 features.

See Missouri Pacific Railroad Station Inset

Jeff Wade, Map 5

Map by Jeff Wade.

from farm to farm before coming to Independence, and after they arrived in 1890, they continued to move around. Bess also moved around in the town, from West Ruby back to her grandparents' home, to the home at 608 North Delaware and then back to 219 North Delaware after her father's suicide.

Another parallel is that both Harry and Bess came from families who had taken considerable risk in their personal financial affairs. Bess's grandfather, George Porterfield Gates, took gambles in his many business pursuits, as did Harry Truman's maternal grandfather, Solomon Young, who was a freighter along the trails. Harry Truman's father, John A. Truman, was also known as someone who took chances. In contrast, Bess's father, David W. Wallace, seemed to be content with working in political patronage positions; however, her mother's family, the Gateses, came from a long line of individuals who were constantly taking risks by investing in new business ventures. However, what served as a stark contrast between the Gates family and the Truman family is the fact that the Gates family realized far more success from their risks than did the Truman family.

There were also some other important differences. If Mary Paxton Keeley's assertion that Independence's social scene was divided along religious lines is correct, the fact that Harry Truman was a Baptist might have been held against him by those who had been lifelong members of the Presbyterian Church or by others who were, in the words of Keeley, at the "top on the pole." However, the question remains a valid one as to why Harry's mother made a decision to send her children to the First Presbyterian Church. Was this an attempt by the Truman family to move up among the social ranks of Independence, or was Martha Ellen Truman just sending her children to the First Presbyterian Church because it was one of the few churches that had a Sunday school? The answer to this question remains elusive; however, the community was indeed divided by religion, which did have an impact on the social circles of both Harry and Bess.

This period was formative in the life of Harry S. Truman. He always talked about the importance of education, and during his presidency, he created the President's Commission on Higher Education. His love of learning and the recognition of the importance of education were fostered in Independence, and he took that importance with him wherever he went for the rest of his life.

Haberdasher and County Judge, 1919–1933

You said I write letters that are no good, well you don't say much in yours. But I'm glad to get them even if there were only an envelope with an address to me, written by you. I am in bed in my old room at the farm, and I can remember how I used to lie up here and wait for a letter from you, and then read the old one. Those were the days—why didn't you marry me when I first asked you? I don't know, do you?[33]
—*Harry to Bess, April 15, 1933*

Between 1902 and 1918, Harry Truman did not officially live in Independence; however, he still had ties to the city because the Noland sisters lived across the street from the Wallace family. Tragedy struck the Wallace family at their home at 608 North Delaware in May 1903. David Wallace, Bess's father, took his own life in the family home. Mary Paxton Keeley recalled that her father woke her up at five o'clock in the morning to tell her the news, and she immediately went over to see Bess. Keeley remembered that "Bess was walking up and down back of the house with clenched hands…She wasn't crying. There wasn't anything I could say, but I just walked up and down with her. I don't remember his funeral. Then Mrs. Wallace told me later that she felt so humiliated."[34]

The Wallace family spent one year in Colorado Springs, Colorado, and returned to Independence, where the family—including Bess and brothers Frank, George and Fred—moved into 219 North Delaware to live with the Gates family. Bess attended the Barstow school in Kansas City and participated in Independence's social scene by going on dates and attending other social functions.

Meanwhile, Harry Truman, upon graduating from Independence High School, held several positions, including timekeeper for the L.J. Smith Company, and he also worked as a bank clerk for Commerce Bank in Kansas City. In 1906, his mother and father, who had left Independence in 1902, asked him to come to the six-hundred-acre Grandview farm to help them manage the operation. While on the farm, he became a partner with his father in the Truman & Son Farming operation, and he kept the books and did everything he could to make the farm a success. Tragedy struck the Truman farm in 1914 when John A. Truman died, which left Harry to work the farm with his mother and sister. It was a tragedy all too familiar to Bess Wallace in Independence.

Harry spent much of his time helping his father with the farming operation, and after 1914, when his father died, he devoted more attention to farm management; however, he had interests that extended beyond the farm. He joined the Farm Bureau, Grandview Commercial Club, Modern Woodmen and the Masonic organization. Of the four, the most important organization he joined was the Masonic organization because he maintained a commitment to the organization for the rest of his life. His most important off-the-farm pursuit was Bess Wallace.[35]

In December 1910, Harry paid a visit to the Noland sisters at 216 North Delaware. As neighbors would do, Madge Wallace had baked a dessert and sent it over to the Nolands. The Noland sisters convinced Harry to return the cake plate across the street to 219 North Delaware. Harry walked across Delaware Street and approached 219 North Delaware. He knocked on the door, and Bess Wallace opened it, allowing the two old Sunday school classmates and Independence High graduates to renew their acquaintance. The return of the cake plate sparked a nine-year courtship between Harry and Bess, and in December 1911, Bess, no doubt with her mother's approval, extended a standing Sunday invitation to Truman to visit her at 219 North Delaware.[36]

From 1910 to 1917, Harry dated Bess by commuting back and forth between Grandview and Independence. It was a short distance of about fifteen miles; however, there was no direct route, and it easily took several hours for Harry to make the journey. He would sometimes spend the night at the Nolands or in Frank Wallace's room at 219 North Delaware if he stayed overnight in Independence. In 1914, he purchased a 1911 Stafford automobile that allowed him to take Bess, her brothers, her brother's dates and the Noland sisters to places in Jackson County. They enjoyed traveling to picnics on the Little Blue River and also going to plays in Kansas City.[37]

The Red Cross awarded this certificate to Bess Wallace for her service in the war effort performed from May 20 to May 25, 1918. *Truman Library.*

In 1917, when the United States entered World War I, the couple's relationship continued exclusively by letter; however, before he left to train at Fort Sill, the two became officially engaged. The Saturday, September 15, 1917 edition of the *Independence Examiner* reported the engagement: "Mrs. David W. Wallace announces the engagement of her daughter, Elizabeth Virginia to Lieutenant Harry S. Truman of the Second Missouri Field Artillery."[38]

Bess's friends responded with congratulatory letters. Mary Ann Sturges wrote:

> *I just want to wish you worlds & worlds of happiness. I do so want to see your ring. Adelaide [Twyman] told me how beautiful it was—engagement rings are always beautiful—aren't they regardless of style or size.*
>
> *Do congratulate Mr. Truman for me—won't you. Wish I might see him—to tell him what a truly fortunate man he is (as if he wasn't aware of the fact.) You know I think there is only one Bess—no one quite exactly like her.*[39]

Harry Truman in his World War I military uniform. *Truman Library.*

Before Harry Truman's service in World War I, he struggled to be successful. Most historians have marked his military career as a turning point in his life. During the war, he became Captain Harry Truman and commanded more than two hundred men in Battery D in France. The unit was responsible for transporting, maintaining and firing four artillery pieces on the battlefield. Most of the men who served in the battery were Irish Catholics from Kansas City, and after the war, when his unit returned home, most of the men in Harry's battery supported him in his business and political ventures for the rest of his life.

When Harry returned from France, he married Bess on June 28, 1919, in the Trinity Episcopal Church in Independence. Madge Gates Wallace started attending the church in 1901, and Bess and her brother Frank were both confirmed in the church in 1903.[40] The local paper described the wedding as one of "unusual beauty and interest" and noted that "Miss Wallace has lived in Independence all her life and has a large circle of friends," while Truman "has spent much time away" though Independence still "claims" him. Bess wore a "lovely gown of white Georgette with hat of white faille and carried Aaron Ward roses," and she was given away by her brother Frank Wallace.[41]

Adelaide Twyman, a close friend of Bess's who lived at 416 North Delaware, sent a letter to her at the Blackstone Hotel in Chicago, Illinois, where the couple spent a night on their way to Detroit for their honeymoon. The letter read:

> *I just hope my epistle will be the first one "Mrs. Harry Truman" will receive. If that honor should befall me, I should feel too stuck up for words...*
>
> *I am still thinking of your lovely wedding, which was by far the sweetest I ever attended. Even the weather was as perfect as the proverbial "day in June" would be and the whole setting was just what it should have been for you. Your attendants looked so pretty and the Captain so wonderful and handsome and, as for the bride—well words fail when I try to tell any feelings for her.*
>
> *I am afraid, Bess, that I shall never be able to tell you how dearly I love you and how much I value your friendship. It certainly means a great deal to me. And knowing what a splendid man your husband is, I feel sure that life will hold for you both the greatest happiness and success. I shall think of you often as you go honey-mooning about and shall look forward to the time when I see you again.*[42]

Bess also received a letter from her sister-in-law, Natalie Ott Wallace, who married her brother Frank in the First Presbyterian Church on April 6, 1915. Bess's other brother, George, married May Southern on October 24, 1916. Both couples moved into two bungalows that were constructed immediately to the east of the George P. Gates home. Frank and Natalie's home, at 601 West Truman Road, was finished in the late summer or early fall of 1915, and George and May's home, located at 605 West Truman Road, was completed by the fall of 1916. Natalie told Bess, "Yesterday was the 'day after' sure enough. Every one sat around half a sleep. Mother is let down...We are taking good care of Mother so stay as long as you want and have a wonderful time because no other time will ever be the same."[43]

While Harry and Bess were courting by letter, he spoke often about providing a place for Bess. However, when the couple returned from their honeymoon, they settled into 219 North Delaware to live with Madge Gates Wallace. This arrangement seemed to suit Madge. Her house, sometimes known as the "Big House," and the two Wallace bungalows just to the east were sometimes collectively referred to as the "Wallace family compound."

When Harry returned home, he decided to open a men's furnishing goods store in downtown Kansas City with army buddy Eddie Jacobson. The two

The Truman wedding party, June 28, 1919. *Front row, left to right*: Helen Wallace, Harry Truman, Bess Truman and Louise Wells. *Back row, left to right*: Ted Marks and Frank Wallace. *Truman Library*.

men called their venture Truman and Jacobson, and the store became a meeting place for his former Battery D members. However, Harry was not just content to manage the store. He became active in a number of civic pursuits, much as he had done on the farm.

KANSAS CITY, MO. *Sept 5.* 19*19*

M⁻ *Harry Truman*

IN ACCOT WITH
TED MARKS, TAILOR
STRICTLY HIGH GRADE TAILORING

221 EAST 10TH STREET
BETWEEN GRAND AND MCGEE

HOME PHONE 5334 MAIN

1	Grey stripe suit	70 00
1	Shepard plaid	65 00
1	Uniform cleaned & pressed	1 25
1	Suit cleaned & pressed (2 pieces)	1 25
1	Raincoat " "	1 50
1	Raincoat pressed	75
1	Uniform pressed	75
1	suit pressed 3 piece	75
4	suits pressed	2 00
4	" " Paid Oct 5/19	2 00
1	suit cleaned & pressed	1 25
1	" pressed	50
		14 00

Ted Marks, who served as Harry Truman's best man in his wedding, also tailored the gray checkered suit he wore that day. *Truman Library.*

Truman and Jacobson advertising blotter. *Truman Library.*

He continued his involvement in the Masons and joined other organizations like the Triangle Club, which was a group of young Kansas City business professionals. He also became active in the American Legion, and in 1921, he served as the vice-chair and sometimes acting chair of the

Decorations Committee. As a member of the decorations committee, he sent letters to the mayor of Kansas City, Kansas, and to the Kansas City (Missouri) School Board to encourage all of their citizens and residents to fly American flags at their places of residence for the American Legion Convention that was held in Kansas City from October 31 to November 2. He also wrote letters to Kansas City merchants and encouraged their businesses to display not only the American flag but also the flags of the Allied countries during the convention. Truman told one business owner, "If the merchants will display allied flags and lots of bunting during the convention, it will make these visiting veterans feel as if they are more than welcome, make them feel that they are still appreciated for winning a great war, and that this town feels honored to have them here."[44]

Part of the convention activities included the dedication of the Liberty Memorial on November 1, 1921, which became the nation's first monument to those who served in World War I. He also organized the Kansas City–area Reserve Officers Club, and according to historian Alonzo Hamby, he remained very active in the organization until 1937. One of his most time-consuming pursuits was his activity as a reserve officer in the Missouri National Guard, which required him to train for at least two weeks out of the year. He began his Reserve Officer Training in 1923 and continued training until he was a senator.[45]

By 1922, Truman and Jacobson struggled to keep the business afloat, and in 1922, it folded. Harry looked for another opportunity. While Truman and Jacobson was still open, Jim Pendergast, army buddy and son of Mike Pendergast (who was the brother of noted Kansas City political boss Thomas J. Pendergast and responsible for the machine's activities in eastern Jackson County), called on Harry at the store with a political offer. The Pendergasts told him that if he decided to run for the position of Eastern District judge of Jackson County, their political organization would support his candidacy. This meeting might have occurred before February 1922 because Harry wrote to a friend, "They are trying to run me for Eastern Judge out at Independence and I guess they'll do it before they get through. It'll be rather soft for the service men if I am on the County Court and Garrett is Mayor of Kansas City, won't it? I know one thing—the court house will look like a D Battery reunion every day if they are foolish enough to send me down there."[46] Truman quickly mulled over the opportunity, and in March 1922, he kicked off his campaign in the Memorial Building in Lee's Summit, Missouri, where he spoke at a meeting that had been arranged by the American Legion post in the town.[47]

Like This Card There Are Two Sides To Every Question

THIS side deals with a local political situation that is personal, as the voter and tax-payer should demand a business administration of county affairs. The past per-formance of the County Court of Jackson County is the best recommendation that can be offered in asking your support for the Eastern County member. If you still desire business methods employed in the handling of county business for the next two years cast your vote on November 4th for

HARRY S. TRUMAN

DEMOCRATIC NOMINEE FOR

JUDGE OF THE COUNTY COURT

EASTERN DISTRICT - JACKSON COUNTY - MISSOURI

This Card Compiled and Paid For By His Friends   90

Campaign card for Truman's Eastern District judge campaign. *Truman Library.*

In Harry's first election, Bess's brother, Frank, who was a Democratic ward boss of the First Ward in Independence, took Harry Truman to the Independence Square and introduced him to the people he knew as they walked. One of those people Harry met in the spring of 1922 was Rufus Burrus, who became a lifelong friend and the family's personal attorney.[48]

In Missouri and Jackson County politics, which were dominated by the Democratic Party, the candidate had to win the August primary in order to have a strong chance at winning the November election. However, the Democratic Party in the county was divided into two important factions: the Goats and the Rabbits. Thomas Pendergast and Harry Truman were affiliated with the Goat faction. One of Harry's old Waldo Avenue Gang members, Henry Chiles, was affiliated with the Rabbits. The Jackson County Court had a presiding judge of the court (elected by a vote of the entire county), a Western District judge (elected by the voters primarily in Kansas City) and an Eastern District judge (who represented Independence and the rural sections of Jackson County). Jackson County employed about nine hundred people, and the three judges made decisions about who would get those jobs, so that is why the Pendergast machine, which usually controlled the presiding judge and Western District judge, encouraged Truman to run for the Eastern District judge position—Pendergast wanted to control all three of the elected positions and all of the political patronage that went along with those elected positions.[49]

The Democratic factions battled it out in the primary to get their candidate elected. Then, in the November election, the Democratic factions would support the Democratic candidate who won the August election. The Democratic faction that lost the August primary was rewarded with half of the county's 900 jobs in exchange for supporting the Democratic candidate who was on the ballot in November. This meant that 450 jobs would go to the Rabbits and 450 jobs would go to the Goats.

In the August primary, Harry Truman faced Rabbit candidate Emmett Montgomery from Blue Springs. In May, Harry ordered some small business cards from the Independence Examiner Printing Company; his largest campaign expenditure was $135, which paid for precinct maps. He defeated Montgomery in the August primary by a vote of 4,230 to 3,951. Apparently, Montgomery's supporters attempted to tamper with one of the ballot boxes in order to win the election; however, Harry's friends became aware of the attempt and stopped it. Because the election was close, Harry thought that Montgomery would ask for a recount. The recount did not take place; however, on August 9, 1922, Harry filed papers of his own with the Jackson County Board of Election Commissioners to challenge the vote if Montgomery pressed for a recount.[50]

After the primary, Harry filed a report with the State of Missouri that listed his total expenditures for the campaign at $519.80.[51] He thanked his supporters and told one of them:

> *I have the opportunity of my lifetime to make a record in that office and I've got to make it because my friends expect it. It was the good boosts from men like you and from my soldier boys that made me win. The victory was gained without money and without the promise of a single job. It has never been done before and I am hoping to show them a lot of things for which there is no precedent.*[52]

He was correct to note the importance that his Battery D boys played in the primary election. They continued to support him in the fall campaign, when more than sixty of his former battery members paid for an advertisement that endorsed his candidacy for the Eastern District judge. The article featured a photograph of a silver cup that Battery D members presented him on June 8, 1919, immediately after they returned to the United States from France. The inscription on the cup read, "Presented by the members of Battery D in appreciation of his justice, ability and leadership." The ad noted that Truman was a "farmer, banker, soldier, and merchant" and that "at these things he has made good. He will make good as Eastern Judge."[53] No mention was made in either the ad or in the campaign of his failed haberdashery.

Harry outlined his political platform in a letter he sent to Carl Jenkins in September:

If I have anything to do with the management of this county's affairs in the next two years there will be a decided change from the present. And if we have the proper management we will have a "business" administration. I expect to be the county's servant just the same as if I were president of a private corporation. I still maintain that the county's business or politics or government as you please will not mix with my private affairs.

It is interesting that his campaign tone was very similar to the national Republican strategy during the 1920s, which could be summed up by one of the pronouncements of Warren Harding, who successfully ran for the presidency in 1920: "Less government in business more business in government."[54]

Harry's first campaign was unlike Harding's strategy in that his campaign resonated with labor unions, a constituency that the Republicans sought to weaken during the 1920s. In October, the Amalgamated Association of Street and Electric Railway Employees of America, Kansas City Local 764, endorsed Truman's candidacy. The union described itself as an organization of about seven hundred, and the endorsement letter told Truman that the union's services were "at your disposal in any manner in which you may see fit to use them."[55]

The campaign took in a number of financial contributions; however, the Pendergast name never appeared on any of these lists. Harry made the largest contribution of $150 and was followed by a contribution of $100 each from John Cook, George Bryant, Independence Hardware and Chrisman-Sawyer.[56]

Fred Baker, William Duke, E.I. Purcell and William Newbanks managed his campaign headquarters, which was located on the Independence Square at 111½ West Lexington. Robert Hood and Charles Latimer oversaw the finances of the campaign, and Arthur S. Metzger and R.J. Lambert were responsible for advertising. Harry established a speakers bureau that included the following men and women: Mrs. John Twyman, John Thice, Mrs. Reese Alexander, Mrs. O.H. Gentry, Mrs. Wherritt, Robert L. Yeager, R.L. Winters and Mrs. Yingling. The campaign also created an extensive list of a dozen individuals who could drive voters to the polls on election day. Harry Abbott provided some evidence that Truman appealed to Republicans in Fairmount, which was just to the north and west of Independence.

Harry Abbott, Pendergast precinct worker in Fairmont, remembered in November 1922 that he operated a carpool to get Democrats to the polls during the election. Abbott told Les Byam, Pendergast leader for Fairmount, that he had Republicans who wanted to vote for Truman and wondered if he could extend his carpool services to them. Byam told Abbott no, and after the election, Abbott stepped down from his position. Abbott estimated Republican support for Harry Truman in Fairmount at three to one.[57]

With Harry's election victory, he set out to make good on his promise to apply business methods to government. By February 1923, he faced opposition to his plans because he refused to appoint some individuals to county government positions. The Fourteenth Precinct Democratic Club in South Englewood wanted a plumber and machinist appointed to two positions; however, Harry told the club, "I want to call your attention to the financial condition of the county. It will be impossible for us to maintain the same establishment as last year and expect to pay any of the deficit left us by the previous court. In order to make expenses meet the anticipated income it was necessary to cut down the payroll and we now only have one plummer [*sic*] and about half the machinists we had last year." W.A. Hill, a neighbor from Grandview, Missouri, wrote a complimentary letter to Harry praising his ability to cut the payroll, and Harry responded by telling Hill:

We are honestly trying to put the county on somewhat of a business basis, but it is an uphill job. We need all the boosts we can get from the taxpayers. We are endeavoring by pursuing a policy of real economy to save enough money to pay the large deficit inherited from past courts. If we can sell all but a few of the many automobiles the county has been maintaining and cut the number of deputies to the number actually needed there is a chance for us to pay out in about four years.

It is my ambition to have a hand in one real business administration for Jackson County. It is not popular with the politicians but one term is all I ran for and that is all I expect to have, but when I go out I expect to leave with a clean record.[58]

The eastern Jackson County judge only served a two-year term, so despite the fact that Harry told Hill that he was only going to serve one term, he decided to run for reelection in 1924. Harry faced Robert Hood from Independence in the August primary and won the election by polling 6,833 votes to Hood's 5,234; however, the Democratic factions began to argue about patronage, and evidence suggests that Harry did not want to honor the fifty/fifty arrangement that required the Goats to award half of the patronage jobs to the Rabbits in exchange for their support in the November election.[59]

In an attempt to not be cut out of the patronage in the November election, the Rabbits and another Democratic faction, the Independents, which had strong ties to the Klan, worked out an agreement with the

Republican candidate for the Eastern District judge, Henry Rummel, who owned a shop on the Independence Square, where they agreed to support his candidacy in exchange for some patronage positions. The political horse trade cost Harry the election, and Rummel defeated him by a vote of 11,587 to 10,721.[60]

Henry Chiles, who did not support Harry in the election because he was allied with the Rabbit political faction, remembered how he and Roger Sermon, the Goat precinct captain and longtime Truman ally, conducted the campaign:

> *I was a precinct captain. The Rabbits they handed me this precinct out here. "Now that's your precinct, now you had better go out and come up with something." And I appointed the judges and clerks, that is, suggested them. I saw that the judges and clerks were there and I stayed at the polls all day. I had a poll list and I had my orders. Funny thing about when Truman was running against Rummel—Roger Sermon, the mayor of Independence, he lived on the next block (he and I grew up together, too). He was the Goat captain and I was the Rabbit captain, and I said, "Roger, I don't know what to do about this. I'm going to have to go against Truman and you are going to be for him." He said, "Well, that's all right."*
>
> *We—Roger and I—had a system we'd have one car to haul the passengers, to haul the voters, and he'd go down one side of the street and I'd go down the other. And we worked all day that way. He was for Truman and I was against him.[61]*

A few days after the election, Harry made arrangements to meet with a friend for dinner at the Kansas City Club. When he arrived, he was greeted by sixty-five men, about half of them Battery D members and the other half composed of his political friends. After dinner, the group presented him a watch that was engraved with the inscription, "Judge Harry S. Truman from his Buddies and Friends, November 18, 1924."[62]

Truman's defeat must have taken him aback and forced him to scramble to find work because he still was paying on his debts from the haberdashery and on debts related to the farm in Grandview. On February 17, 1924, Harry and Bess Truman became parents when Mary Margaret was born in an upstairs bedroom of 219 North Delaware. Margaret was a welcome sight to the Wallace family compound and instantly became a favorite of her aunts, May and Natalie Wallace, and her aunts across the street, Nellie and Ethel Noland, all of whom never had any children of their own.

Bess's world revolved around Independence and 219 North Delaware, especially after the birth of Margaret. Glimpses of what her life was like during this period can be obtained by closely examining some of the letters that she wrote to Harry while he was away for two weeks at either Fort Leavenworth in 1923 or Fort Riley, Kansas, from 1925 to 1931, while attending the Missouri National Guard encampment. In 1932, he was promoted to the rank of colonel in command of the 379th Field Artillery, which he held until 1935, when he became a U.S. senator.[63] Harry enjoyed his two weeks in camp because it allowed him the opportunity to get away from all of the job seekers and contractors who wanted either

Bess Truman and baby Margaret, circa 1924. *Truman Library.*

jobs or contracts with the county government; however, that did not always stop them from trying to contact him while he was away. In July 1923, Bess told Harry, "Just one woman has hollered about roads this week."[64]

On the other hand, these two-week absences did not always sit well with Bess, especially after Margaret's birth. In 1925, the encampment moved to Fort Riley, which was much farther away than Fort Leavenworth. In July 1925, Bess wrote to Harry about Margaret, "Frank & Natalie took Margaret for a long ride this evening then she came home, ate and went straight to sleep. She slept all night last night on the sleeping porch—and waked up the minute the sun struck her—about five o'clock! I brought her in at 5:30—she was up parading around her bed by that time."[65]

In that same letter, Bess raised an important issue that dominated the letters exchanged between the two during this period. The 1920s was noted for the emergence of the modern woman who sported bobbed hair. Bess told Harry that his cousin, Nellie Noland, "had her hair cut" and that "she looks perfectly fine." She then informed him that his other cousin, Ethel, was also going to get her hair cut. Then she asked him, "Why won't you agree enthusiastically? My hair grows so fast, I could soon put it up again if it looked very badly—Please!—I'm much more conspicuous having long hair than I will be with it short."[66]

On July 8, Bess informed him that Ethel Noland, his cousin across the street, had cut her hair and that "she looks great." She asked Harry, "When may I do it? I never wanted to do anything as badly in my life. Come on, be a sport. Ask all the married men in camp about their wives' heads & I'll bet anything I have there isn't one under sixty who has long hair."

Truman responded to her request, "Say, if you want your hair bobbed so badly go on and get it done. I want you to be happy regardless of what I think about it. I am very sure you'll be just as beautiful with it off and I'll not say anything to make you sorry for doing it. I can still see you as the finest on earth so go and have it done. I've never been right sure you weren't kidding me anyway. You usually do as you like about things and that's what I want you to do."[67]

Harry Truman was county judge when the community decided to construct the Memorial Building, which served as a community building, as well as a memorial for veterans of the Spanish-American War and World War I. The building also served as Harry Truman's polling place. *Truman Library.*

PROGRAM

MASTER OF CEREMONIES
Herbert C. Van Smith, Commander, Tirey J. Ford Post

Overture, Walnut Park Orchestra, Orlando Nace, Conductor

"America the Beautiful"..........L. D. S. Messiah Choir
Paul N. Craig, Director

Invocation........................Rev. J. E. Alexander

Medley of Patriotic Airs.......................The Choir

History ....Mayor Roger T. Sermon

Eulogy and Dedication............Rev. Earl A. Blackman

Anthem.................................... The Choir

Introduction........................Col. E. M. Stayton

Address..................Col. L. J. Van Schaik, U. S. A.

"Long, Long Trail" ....The Choir

Benediction........................Rev. A. G. Clohessy

"The Star Spangled Banner"..........,.Entire Assemblage

CITY'S ADVISORY COMMITTEE	CITY COUNCIL
	MAYOR—Roger T. Sermon
W. C. Dunn, Sr.	COUNCILMEN—1924, 1925, 1926, 1927

CITY'S ADVISORY COMMITTEE	CITY COUNCIL	
W. C. Dunn, Sr.	W. Logan Jones	G. C. Stewart
A. L. Wilson	T. R. Chandler	A. K. Dillee
N. D. Jackson	E. R. Humphrey	J. A. McCurdy
Mize Peters	R. J. Lambert	J. C. Noel
George A. Gould	B. M. Houchens	J. R. Jones
M. H. Siegfried	L. A. Harbin	I. R. Lynch
Harry A. Sturges	H. H. Davis	Chas. C. Koehler
Edgar Hinde		

DEDICATION COMMITTEE

Harry S. Truman	Kenneth V. Bostian
Spencer Salisbury	Harry A. Sturges

Radiocast KLDS 440.9 Meters
Piano by T. J. Watkins Music Company
Decorations by Wyandote Tent and Awning Company
Printed by Swan Printing Company, Independence, Missouri

The dedication program for the Memorial Building. *Truman Library.*

From December 1924 to August 1926, according to historian Richard Lawrence Miller, in order to provide for his family, Harry sold memberships in the Kansas City Automobile Club, which served as a social club in addition to providing free towing to members. The organization was headquartered at Tenth and Central in Kansas City and maintained a clubhouse in Hickman Mills, located in south Kansas City. He remained active in the club and sold memberships until 1926. In addition to selling automobile memberships, he became involved in the Community Savings and Loan Association in 1925 when he sold stock in the company to potential investors. Harry also became involved in another company, Truman-Barr Insurance Agency, which was affiliated with the Community Savings and Loan venture.[68]

In November 1926, the members of the National Old Trails Road Association elected him president of the organization. The mission of the organization was to encourage state and federal governments to construct roads that followed the overland trails once used by Native Americans and American settlers. The organization partnered with the Daughters of the American Revolution (DAR) to honor communities along the old trails that contributed to the settlement of the West. Representatives from the National Old Trails organization and the DAR traveled the country and dedicated Pioneer Mother statues. In April 1928, Harry traveled to Washington, D.C. In September 1928, he presided over the dedication of a Pioneer Mother statue at Lexington, Missouri.[69]

Harry, with Pendergast's blessing, cast his hat back into the political ring in 1926 when he announced his candidacy for the presiding judge position

Harry Truman was a lifelong member of the National Old Trails Road Association. *Truman Library.*

Margaret, Harry and Bess Truman in the backyard of 219 North Delaware, May 1928. *Truman Library.*

of Jackson County, which would be decided by all of the voters in Jackson County, not just those in eastern Jackson County. This also meant that Pendergast could deliver more votes to him because he controlled most of the polling wards in Kansas City. In contrast to previous elections, where the political battle was waged in the August primary, as Richard Lawrence Miller noted, Truman had no opposition to his candidacy for presiding judge in the August primary. The reason for this was that Thomas Pendergast, leader of the Goats, and Joseph Shannon, leader of the Rabbits, had patched up their political differences, and Harry easily cruised to a victory in November.[70]

According to Jennie Johnson, whose husband was "Tiny" Clark Johnson, the political arrangement when her husband became a bailiff in 1929 was that two-thirds of the patronage positions went to Pendergast and the remaining one-third went to Shannon. She also revealed that there were certain departments within the county government that were controlled by the various factions. She remembered that the Goats controlled the treasurer's office and the tax office, while the Rabbits controlled the sheriff's office and the probate court.[71]

In that same election, Harry's Latin teacher, Ardelia Hardin Palmer, was elected to the position of Independence city assessor, which was the first time that a woman held elected office in Independence. When Palmer was elected to the position, Independence did not have office space for the assessor, and Harry invited her to come over to the Jackson County Courthouse to establish an office there. Palmer remembered what Harry told her: "You come on in to the county court's office and use our desks, because we are not there half the time." She continued:

> *So, I wrote my books up there in the courthouse in the office where Harry Truman was Presiding judge, and when Harry would come over, if we ever had a minute together, he would want to talk. He wanted to talk about the "War Between the States" and about my father Hopkins Hardin, who was in Pickett's Charge at Gettysburg…*
>
> *Several times my father was asked to come to the high school in those days and talk to Miss Margaret Phelps' history class about his experiences in the War Between the States. I can remember that Harry would tell me how he considered General Robert E. Lee a great hero. Well, Harry and I had some happy hours together at the courthouse when he was judge of the county court and I city assessor for Independence. I was city assessor from 1926 to 1936.[72]*

Ardelia Palmer was a firm believer in Harry Truman, and in 1928, she organized the Jackson Democratic Club, which was a group of Independence women that supported Democratic candidates running for political office. The organization remained active until it was absorbed into the Women's Jackson Democratic Club in about 1952.

As presiding judge of Jackson County, Harry had more political influence than he had when he was a county judge for the Eastern District. He came into the position, according to Richard Miller, with

> *a vision of the future and of what Jackson County government should do to improve the lives of its citizens. Such vision among politicians is unusual; even more extraordinary was the ability Truman would demonstrate in implementing these plans. No misty dreamer, he had the savvy needed to accomplish these goals. In the next eight years he would prove himself to be no mere administrator, but a leader of fellow citizens, convincing them that his vision should be theirs, showing the paths that had to be used, and bringing them safely along those paths to the sought-after goals.[73]*

Those "sought-after goals" included Harry's commitment to building a quality road system for the county. While he was dating Bess, he learned firsthand the importance of quality roads when he, on more than one occasion, made the journey from Grandview to Independence over roads that were less than passable. According to one biographer, "From the day he took office, Truman pursued one overriding objective, the building of a modern highway system for rural-small town Jackson County." Within three weeks of taking office, Harry had hired E.M Stayton, a Democrat and former military associate, and Republican N.T. Veatch to develop a road plan for the county. This was nothing new for Stayton, whom Harry had tasked with drafting a plan to improve and maintain the existing roads during his first term as Eastern District judge. Stayton and Veatch produced a plan that went much further than maintaining and improving the existing roads; they drafted a plan that advocated the construction of 34 miles of asphalt roads and 190 miles of concrete roads. Their goal, shared by Harry, was to create a network of roads in Jackson County that would allow every farmer in the county to be "within two miles of a hard-surfaced road."[74]

A big challenge to implementing the plan was securing county support, but there was also the funding—the plan drafted by Stayton and Veatch was estimated to cost $6.5 million. Harry obtained the support of the Taxpayers League, which was headed by Marvin Gates, another military associate; the Kansas City Chamber of Commerce, led by another friend, Lou Holland; and the Kansas City Public Service Institute, led by Walter Matscheck.

With the support of these local institutions, Harry then took his road building campaign directly to the voters of Jackson County. He told them that instead of maintaining the existing road system, it would be cost effective in the long run to invest in the Stayton and Veatch plan. He also told his constituents that Stayton and Veatch would oversee the contracting process for the road building plan in order to keep graft and corruption under control. Harry proposed that voters approve a bond issue to fund the road improvement plan, and on May 8, 1928, Harry Truman's birthday, voters went to the polls and approved a huge $31 million package that included money to implement the road building project and also money to construct a county hospital. Harry was elated, and the first contracts for road construction were arranged in September 1928.[75]

According to historian Robert H. Ferrell, the Jackson County Court built 244 miles of road. On May 26, 1931, voters approved a second bond issue that continued the road building project but also approved projects that remodeled the Jackson County Courthouse on the Independence Square and constructed a brand-new courthouse in downtown Kansas City. Harry tapped his brother-in-law, Fred Wallace, who was associated with Keene and Simpson, architects, to serve as the architect for the

Left to right: Thomas Bash, judge, Western District, 1929–30; Robert W. Barr, judge, Eastern District, 1927–30; Howard Vrooman, judge, Western District, 1927–28; Eugene I. Purcell, judge, Eastern District, 1931–32; Presiding Judge Harry S. Truman; W.O. Beeman, judge, Western District, 1931–32. The photo was taken at the "Road Celebration" barbecue at Sni-A-Bar Farm in Jackson County, Missouri, October 12, 1932. *Truman Library.*

Independence remodeling project, and after a whirlwind tour of courthouses, he selected architect Edward T. Neild, who had designed a courthouse in Shreveport, Louisiana, to draft plans for what became the "twenty-eight story, three-hundred-foot-high, $4 million art deco" courthouse in downtown Kansas City.[76]

The *Examiner* described in detail the materials that were used in the construction of the Independence Courthouse and also how it was constructed. The Weeks Construction Company received the overall contract for the project. United Brick and Tile Company of Kansas City furnished the red colonial brick. The Mayor Brick Company of Kansas City provided the Indiana limestone that was used to trim the building and the Bedford cut stone that was used for the columns on the north and south porticos. The *Examiner* described in detail the placement of the columns:

> *Each column was set up in three sections, each ten feet long, three feet in diameter and weighing five tons. These sections were put in place by one*

Remodeling of the Independence Courthouse under the leadership of Presiding Judge Harry Truman, 1933. *Truman Library.*

of the largest pieces of machinery manufactured for the purpose. The boom reached the top of the building and picked up the sections like a feather and put them in place and adjusted them to the fraction of an inch. The portico was completed with the artistic roof resting on the four columns.

Also, two Independence businesses, A.J. Bundschu and Tucker's Furniture, provided the linoleum and the new office furniture for the building, respectively.[77]

On September 7, 1933, Harry hosted an all-day rededication of the Independence Courthouse amid much fanfare. At 9:00 a.m., the festivities began with the finals for the girls' city championship. A parade followed at 9:30 a.m. that started at Alton and Noland Streets and ended at the reviewing stand in front of the Memorial Building. The dedication ceremony began at 2:00 p.m., and the featured speaker was Governor Guy Park, who spoke on the south side of the courthouse steps.

After Park's speech, Harry delivered an address of his own: "Here is your Courthouse finished and furnished within the budget set aside to build it." The county judge then gave a brief overview of county government and listed his accomplishments since 1923, when he served as Eastern District judge. The dedication ceremony concluded with Margaret Truman and Roger T. Sermon, son of Mayor Sermon, unveiling two of the dedication tablets provided by Johnson & Sons Monument Company that were placed on either side of the south entrance to the courthouse. The green marble tablet on the west side gave a brief history of the county, and the tablet on the east listed the composition of the county court and the architects who were involved with the project, including Fred Wallace.[78]

Later that evening, Blevins Davis directed a pageant that he had written that portrayed the history of the county. The pageant featured more than 350 people, and it was performed in the Memorial Building. The *Examiner* estimated that more than 40,000 people attended the dedication events, with about 20,000 people coming from the surrounding towns.[79]

While overseeing these projects consumed much of his time as presiding judge of Jackson County, Harry also had time for several other related pursuits. In 1930, the Missouri State Planning Association appointed him as its chair, and he also was elected to the board of the National Conference on City Planning.[80] By the mid-1930s, Jackson County, the state of Missouri and the nation were beginning to feel the impact of the Great Depression. On November 1, 1933, Harry, with the support of Missouri's entire Democratic Congressional delegation and senior senator, Bennett "Champ" Clark, was appointed director of the Federal Reemployment Service in Missouri.[81]

As Federal Reemployment Service director, Harry established "a system of local employment bureaus" that registered the jobless, certified their eligibility for government relief and attempted to place the workers "in either government work programs or private openings." Historian Alonzo Hamby noted that his work as a director "enhanced Truman's name recognition and enlarged his network of acquaintances around the state" and also allowed him the opportunity to work directly with Franklin Roosevelt's New Deal leaders like Harry Hopkins. Harry resigned his position as director when he announced on May 14, 1934, that he would seek election to the U.S. Senate.[82]

Tom Pendergast, Kansas City political boss, had agreed to support Harry's candidacy; however, Harry did not take the election for granted and campaigned in every county in the state. He even traveled to Missouri's boot heel to meet voters and ask for their support. On July 6, 1934, he was injured in an automobile wreck when another vehicle struck the Plymouth in which he was riding. He was thrown into the windshield, and his ribs hit the gearshift. Undaunted, he continued on to deliver his speech at Jefferson City.[83]

The campaign came to a close in Independence on August 6, 1934, when Harry delivered an evening speech in Independence at the RLDS campus, which was an outdoor amphitheater. Earlier in the day, a bus decorated with streamers and playing band music toured most of the cities and towns in Jackson County, with Truman Senate campaign staffers onboard who

Harry Truman's campaign car, 1934. *Truman Library.*

encouraged people to come to the evening speech. The meeting, which started at 8:00 p.m., was chaired by Independence mayor Roger Sermon. More than four thousand people jammed into the amphitheater in the midst of the Great Depression. Harry told the crowd that "the farmer must be put on a parity with industry before this country may expect to return to a condition of economic prosperity." He also told the crowd that he was interested in "the old age pension movement" because, in his words, "many of these old people face disaster through no fault of their own. I will work for this if I go to Washington." He called on Congress to pay a bonus for veterans who had served in World War I and concluded the speech by saying that he was very pleased that his "home town and home county" had turned out to hear him.[84]

The next day, August 7, 1934, was election day, and the voters went to the polls. Harry dropped by the election board offices around 8:00 p.m., where the workers told him that the initial returns looked good for Jackson County. He returned home and went to bed. When he got up the next morning, he went to his office at the Independence Courthouse, where he listened to the final returns coming in over the radio and took congratulations from those who dropped by and those who called on the phone. By midmorning, it was clear that he had won the primary over three other Democratic challengers.

Later in the day, he told the *Independence Examiner*, "It is impossible for me to express adequately my appreciation to my own county friends and my thanks for what they have done for me. I do not see how it would be possible to receive a finer endorsement. If elected senator I shall serve the state to the best of my ability."[85]

The editor of the *Independence Examiner*, Colonel William Southern, who was the father of Harry's sister-in-law, May Wallace, ran the following editorial:

> *Independence rejoices in the nomination of Judge Harry S. Truman for the Senate. That he will be elected is a foregone conclusion.*
>
> *Judge Truman is a young man, just turned fifty, he is a practical man of experience in dealing with people and is a straight thinker. Judge Truman is not handicapped by years of Washington and the Washington atmosphere and the traditions of Congress. He goes to Washington free from the alliances which so often make members of Congress useless. Judge Truman is a man of high ideals and we shall hear from his work.*
>
> *In the New Deal almost all the old methods and prejudices have been thrown overboard and fresh blood is badly needed. Orators are no longer the great men of the Senate. The Senate is no longer a "Rich Man's Club." If it were, Judge Truman would be mighty lonesome.*
>
> *We are particularly pleased that the Democrats outstate, the men and women in the small County districts gave Judge Truman such fine support. Without this support he could not have been nominated. He is from birth and training and experience a country man as contrasted with those who have never left the sidewalks and the shadow of tall buildings.*
>
> *The nomination of Judge Truman is remarkable in several ways. Unknown in the outstate districts and known not at all in St. Louis, his campaign was entirely in the country and wherever he went he made friends and supporters. The campaign demonstrated another thing. The Democrats of Missouri did not like the idea of a man they had honored highly and whom they had nominated and elected to the United States Senate coming back at the next election and trying to dictate the selection of his colleague.*[86]

In the fall election, held on November 6, 1934, Truman faced Republican opponent Roscoe Patterson. He continued to campaign in the fall, and on election night, he received assurances by late in the evening that he had won. He remarked, "I naturally am very happy at the outcome. I will do my best to be a good public servant. I am deeply grateful to my home people and to my other friends throughout the state. I believe this is all I need to say."[87]

Harry S Truman Historic District National Historic Landmark

Independence, Missouri

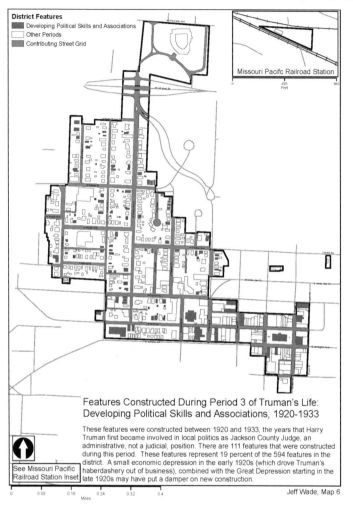

District Features

- Developing Political Skills and Associations
- Other Periods
- Contributing Street Grid

Missouri Pacifc Railroad Station

Features Constructed During Period 3 of Truman's Life:
Developing Political Skills and Associations, 1920-1933

These features were constructed between 1920 and 1933, the years that Harry Truman first became involved in local politics as Jackson County Judge, an administrative, not a judicial, position. There are 111 features that were constructed during this period. These features represent 19 percent of the 594 features in the district. A small economic depression in the early 1920s (which drove Truman's haberdashery out of business), combined with the Great Depression starting in the late 1920s may have put a damper on new construction.

See Missouri Pacific Railroad Station Inset

Jeff Wade, Map 6

Map by Jeff Wade.

William Southern editorialized:

> *Independence has never in the history of the state furnished a member of the United States Senate. When Judge Harry S. Truman takes his seat in the Senate in January this oversight will be corrected.*

63

Harry S Truman Historic District National Historic Landmark

Independence, Missouri

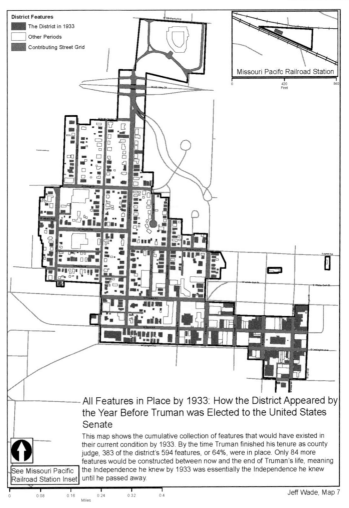

All Features in Place by 1933: How the District Appeared by the Year Before Truman was Elected to the United States Senate

This map shows the cumulative collection of features that would have existed in their current condition by 1933. By the time Truman finished his tenure as county judge, 383 of the district's 594 features, or 64%, were in place. Only 84 more features would be constructed between now and the end of Truman's life, meaning the Independence he knew by 1933 was essentially the Independence he knew until he passed away.

Jeff Wade, Map 7

Map by Jeff Wade.

We congratulate Judge Truman with the certainty that in his wider service at Washington his home town and his home state will always be proud of his work and always glad to say to those on the outside that he is from Independence, Missouri.

If the vote of Jackson County were thrown out entirely the balance of the state would have elected Judge Truman. Nevertheless his home town and his home county gave him a wonderful endorsement. Eastern Jackson County where he has lived and where he was educated gave him four to one and Independence a little higher percentage. This would indicate that he had the support of the Democrats and that a great many Republicans joined to elect a home man.[88]

On the day after the election, a reporter conducted a rare interview with Bess Truman at 219 North Delaware. She told the reporter that she was "thrilled to be going to Washington, but I have spent all my life here on Delaware street and it certainly will be a change." She added that Margaret had stayed up until 1:00 a.m. listening to the returns on the radio. During the interview, a neighbor appeared at the door and told her, "We certainly will miss you, and Delaware won't seem the same in the years you are at Washington."[89]

U.S. Senator and Vice President, 1934-1945

We had a big dinner, to celebrate Harry's having been elected senator, down at the Christian Church; his mother was to talk about him as a boy, I was to talk about him as a pupil. We all had our places; I was sitting by Mrs. Martha Truman that night.[90]
—Mrs. Ardelia Hardin Palmer, Harry Truman's high school Latin teacher

It is a great honor you have brought to Delaware street and we want you to know that we are very proud of you.[91]
—Mr. and Mrs. Olney Burrus to Truman family on Truman's vice presidential nomination, July 23, 1944

Three Democratic clubs, including the Women's Jackson Club, the Junior Jefferson Club and the Young Men's Democratic Club, organized a "home farewell dinner" for the Trumans on December 17, 1934, at the First Christian Church in Independence. What was interesting is that the program featured a speaker who described Harry's life experience as a student at Independence High School, an officer in the U.S. military, his role in the Masonic organization, the work he completed with the National Old Trails Road Association and his experience as a county judge. After the speeches were made, Mayor Roger Sermon presented the Trumans with a luggage set, which included a small bag for Margaret. Harry Truman responded and said, "There is nothing I can say which would adequately express to you my gratitude and appreciation. I cannot by any means tell you how we appreciate this. It is too much to expect. All that I can say is that I will do my best."[92]

Menu

Shrimp Cocktail		Crispy Crackers
Celery	Radishes	Olives
Roast Turkey	Dressing	Giblet Gravy
	Cranberry Sauce	
Brabant Potatoes		Asparagus Tips
	"The Initial" Salad	
Hot Rolls		Preserves
Ice Cream		Angel Food Cake
	Coffee	

Program

Toastmaster..Mr. William Southern, Jr.
Invocation..The Rev. Lawrence M. Proctor
Ensembles—
    Mrs. Fred Liddy, violin; Miss Dorothy Monday, cello;
    Miss Elizabeth Smith, harp; Miss Elizabeth Clinton, piano
Vocal Solo...Mr. Herbert Fraher
    Mrs. Daisy Underwood, accompanist
Piano Solo...Miss Nadine Werner

TOASTS

"The Country Lad"...Mrs. Martha Truman
"School Days"...Mrs. W. L. C. Palmer
"Masonic Affiliations"......................................Mr. G. C. Marquis
"In the A. E. F."..Gen. E. M. Stayton
"Old Trails"...Mrs. Henry Chiles
"County Court—1923 and 1924"..................Judge H. F. McElroy
"County Court—1927 to 1934"
    ....Judge E. I. Purcell and Judge Battle McCardle
"As a Campaigner"..Mr. James P. Aylward
"The Seventy-fourth Congress"..........Congressman C. Jasper Bell
"An Independence Citizen"..................Mayor Roger T. Sermon
"Response".....................................Senator Harry S. Truman
      "Auld Lang Syne"

"Home farewell dinner" program for the Trumans, December 17, 1934. *Truman Library.*

On December 27, 1934, Harry and Margaret traveled to downtown Kansas City, where he dedicated the Kansas City Courthouse. Margaret unveiled the Andrew Jackson statue before the crowd. The next morning, on December 28, 1934, Harry got up and made his way to the county courthouse one last time before departing for Washington. He said his final farewells, and at noon, Harry, Bess and Margaret departed by car for St. Louis, where they boarded a train heading to Washington. Hunter Allen and Bill Cleveland drove the "small car Judge Truman used for his campaign and Mrs. Truman's car" on to Washington.[93]

Leaving Independence had to have been a bittersweet decision for the Truman family. For the most part, with the exception of the time Harry spent in the Reserves during the 1920s, he had not spent any extended time away from the city since his service in World War I. Bess and Margaret spent some time away from Independence in 1933 due in part to Margaret's poor health, which improved when she recovered in a milder climate in Biloxi, Mississippi.

Margaret was only ten years old when the family moved to Washington, and the move had an impact on her. She left behind many neighborhood friends—especially the Henhouse Hicks. This group was similar to Harry's Waldo Avenue Gang. The Hicks included Betty and Sue Ogden, who lived at

612 West Maple, which later burned in a fire, and Marie, Harriet, Mona Jean "Monie" and Barbara Allen, all of whom lived at 616 West Maple. Others were included, but these girls lived the closest to 219 North Delaware. The group of girls liked to scavenge the basements and attics of their respective homes to come up with unique props for neighborhood plays. Barbara Allen Gard, who was the youngest of the group, recalled what Margaret's departure meant to her sisters: "I remember my sisters feeling upset about Marg leaving, and I think it must have been very hard."[94]

During the Senate years, beginning in 1939, from January to May, Margaret attended Gunston Hall, a private school for girls in Washington, D.C. Bess and Margaret usually returned from Washington to Independence in June, and from August to December, Margaret attended the public schools in Independence, which included the Bryant School, Independence Junior High and, eventually, William Chrisman High School. She graduated from Gunston Hall in June 1942.[95]

Harry left behind the Harpie Club, which included Jackson County political associates and former members of Battery D, as well as others he had met in Independence. The Harpie Club met in the residences of its members and in some businesses after hours on the Independence Square to play poker and drink. Bess left behind her Tuesday Bridge Club, which met every two weeks; two members who were closest with her were Natalie and May Wallace, her sister-in-laws. The relationships that Harry and Bess cultivated through these groups continued for the rest of their lives.

On January 3, 1935, Vice President John Nance Garner administered the oath of office to Harry S. Truman, officially making him a U.S. senator from Missouri. The Tirey J. Ford post of the American Legion in Independence sent Harry a brief letter of congratulations to "its most distinguished member." The new senator worked hard during his first six months and tried to stay out of the limelight.[96]

Unfortunately, some of his fellow senators did not welcome him with open arms. Some of them, like his constituents, believed that he was the "Senator from Pendergast." Harry returned to Independence for the first time as a U.S. senator for a brief visit on June 7, 1935; however, he quickly returned to Washington and grew homesick, especially when his anniversary date of June 28 rolled around. He wrote to Bess, "This is the day sixteen years ago that I made a plunge and took a chance for which I have been a better man. My only regret is that it was not done ten years sooner…I have found time to think of you and write you every day. I wonder if you are now or ever have been sorry you did it on June 28, 1919."[97]

Senator Harry Truman on the steps of the Capitol. *Truman Library.*

Their relationship seemed to be the same as it was when they were dating. Harry and Bess exchanged letter after letter from June until August 1935, when Bess and Margaret returned to Washington. Bess and Margaret returned to Independence in December after Margaret's school ended, and the letters started again. Harry returned home for a brief period during the holidays, but he had returned to Washington by January 1, 1936, leaving Bess, Margaret and Madge behind until Margaret's school started. Bess and Margaret had made their way to Washington by the end of January; however, Madge stayed behind to manage the home at 219. Vietta Garr, the family's African American domestic worker, also stayed behind and managed the household.

In addition to Vietta Garr, Fred Wallace, Bess Truman's youngest brother, was also living in the home with his wife, Christine Marion Meyer, who he married in Carmel, California, on July 27, 1933. The couple had two children, David Frederick Wallace Jr., who was born on October 30, 1934, and daughter Marion Wallace, born on March 2, 1937. Fred and Christine called 219 North Delaware home until 1942, when the family moved to Colorado, where Fred worked for the War Production Board, the architectural firm of T.H. Buell and Company and the Colorado State Highway Department. Charlotte Margaret ("Margo") Wallace was born to the couple in Colorado on August 12, 1948.

In April 1936, Madge informed Bess about the work that was being done by Lester around 219 North Delaware. Madge told her daughter that they were working on the garden and that she was going to "get a few plants of the Heavenly Blue Moon time for the back porch." She also wrote about sending some of Vietta's "good vegetable soup to Mrs. Noland & Ethel at noon." They both were apparently ill. In April 1936, Madge told her daughter, "I am getting awfully homesick for you all."[98]

Harry and Bess spent their seventeenth anniversary apart in June 1936 because he had to travel to Philadelphia for the Democratic National convention, where the delegates selected Franklin Roosevelt as their presidential candidate. Harry returned to Washington on June 28, their anniversary, and found himself all alone, as Bess and Margaret had returned to Independence for the summer.

Harry sat down and wrote Bess a love letter. "I hope you are enjoying the day. It's just about as hot here as it was in Independence June 28, 1919. I wish I had a gray-checked suit to celebrate in, but I haven't so put on a white one. There is no special prize for seventeen years of married life that I could discover, so you'll have to make out without any. I'd like to be there to take you out to dinner though. Lots of water has gone under the bridge since then."[99]

Harry returned home in December 1936 for the holidays, but he quickly returned to Washington in early January 1937; however, this time, Bess and Margaret did not follow. In fact, from January to May 1937, Bess and Margaret remained behind in Independence. In January 1937, Harry received a delegation from Independence in Washington that included Roger Sermon and Polly Compton, a fellow neighbor who lived on North Delaware. He told Bess that he took them to lunch and wrote, "I think they enjoyed it."[100]

In 1937, Harry found himself very much involved in the work of the Senate. Late in December 1936, Burton K. Wheeler, chairman of the Interstate Commerce Committee, established a subcommittee to look into America's railroads. The railroads suffered tremendously during the depression, and Wheeler and the committee wanted to understand why. Wheeler appointed Harry to the subcommittee, and in May 1937, he served as acting chair of the committee. He held hearing after hearing, and the work was exhausting.[101]

Bess and Margaret returned to Washington in June 1937 and seemingly remained there through August, as Bess exchanged a steady stream of letters during this time with her mother, who remained in Independence. Harry was pleased to have both Bess and Margaret around; however, by September 1937, the stress of the job had gotten to him. The year had been challenging enough. In addition to Harry's work on Wheeler's subcommittee, he supported President Roosevelt's court-packing scheme, which the president pushed in order to expand the size of the court so he could appoint justices who would support the New Deal. The attempt failed; however, it was not the only political challenge that Harry faced during that time.

Back home in Kansas City, the Pendergast machine that supported his candidacy was showing its first signs of stress. The governor of Missouri, Lloyd Stark, and Thomas Pendergast were political allies; however, in 1937, that relationship slowly began to unravel as Stark began to back away from supporting the machine. There was one additional local concern, and it was a personal one. The Grandview farm, where Harry's mother and sister lived, faced foreclosure, and Harry tried to stop it. The local political situation and farm mortgage, coupled with the long absences from Bess and Margaret, took their toll, and in September 1937, he drove himself to Hot Springs, Arkansas, for evaluation and treatment. He arrived on September 11 and departed on September 23. He told his doctors that he suffered from headaches. They gave him a battery of tests, including an eye exam, which revealed that his astigmatism in his eyes had worsened.[102]

The doctor encouraged him to get more physical exercise. Later in life, Harry claimed that his morning walks began when he became a senator in

1935; however, the evidence suggests that they began after his visit to Hot Springs in 1937 because letters that he wrote to Bess in December 1937 indicate that he was taking a morning walk in Washington, D.C.[103]

Harry spent about a week and a half in Hot Springs, and by late October and November, he found himself alone again in Washington. He continued to hold hearings on the condition of America's railroads. He told Bess in November 1937, "This so-called committee work is nothing but drudgery and publicity, all so depressing sometimes. I'm not so sure that even after I've aired all the Missouri Pacific dirty linen that anything but another chance to dirty some more will come of it."[104]

On Sunday, December 5, 1937, he sat down and fired off another letter to Bess, telling her, "Today is my father's birthday. He'd be eighty-six if he'd lived. I always wished he'd lived to see me elected to this place. There'd have been no holding him." Harry returned to Independence for the holidays, and then, in January 1938, he returned to Washington, with Bess and Margaret accompanying him this time.[105]

The spring of 1938 was a busy time for the senator, who continued to work on the Senate subcommittee. He also, along with Senator Wheeler, began drafting legislation that would strengthen the railroad industry. Harry and Wheeler found out that the railroad companies did not struggle because they paid their workers too much, but rather because the managers of the railroads were not effective.[106]

Back home in Missouri, the attorney for the Western District of the state, Maurice Milligan, was up for reappointment. Milligan had distinguished himself by initiating a federal grand jury to look at vote fraud in the 1936 election that was held in Kansas City. Harry took to the floor of the Senate and denounced Milligan; however, this completely backfired against him. As Alonzo Hamby noted, by the end of 1938, Milligan had indicted 278 people and secured sixty-three convictions.[107]

Harry thought that Milligan's indictments and convictions directly threatened Kansas City's Pendergast machine, and he was right. Unfortunately, that was the least of Harry's worries. Franklin Roosevelt and some of the advisors around him had become increasingly concerned about the corruption in Kansas City because it was well publicized in the United States, and he was concerned that it would focus negative attention on the Democratic Party. Even though Harry had been a loyal New Dealer, Roosevelt had great concern about his connection with the machine, and the relationship between Truman and Roosevelt was strained from 1938 to August 1940, when the Democratic primary for Truman's Senate reelection was held.

By the time of the August 1940 primary, the Pendergast machine was fading from political power. On January 23, 1939, the U.S. attorney for the Western District of Missouri asked a federal judge to convene a federal grand jury to look into the possibility that Tom Pendergast failed to pay income taxes on an insurance payoff, and on April 7, 1939, Good Friday, the grand jury returned a two-count indictment for income tax evasion against Pendergast. On May 22, 1939, Thomas Pendergast appeared in court and, in a deal worked out with Milligan, who was prepared to bring additional charges against him, pleaded guilty to the two counts. Federal judge Otis sentenced Pendergast, and he entered Leavenworth Federal Penitentiary on May 29, 1939, serving one year of time before being released on May 30, 1940.[108]

Harry watched all of this unfold from a distance in Washington. Bess and Margaret were with him from January to June 1939, when they returned to 219 North Delaware. In contrast, he stayed as far away from the situation as possible and maintained a low profile. In July 1939, he informed Bess that he had succeeded in placing the railroad bill on the Senate calendar. On September 6, 1939, France and Great Britain declared war on Germany after the German invasion of Poland, and the Second World War began. It was also in September that Governor Stark announced that he would challenge Harry Truman in the 1940 Senate race. Harry was almost too busy to notice because in November he took a trip to Latin America as part of the Military Subcommittee of the Appropriations Committee to tour military installations in Mexico, Nicaragua, San Salvador and Guatemala. In December, he inspected Moffett Field at the southern end of San Francisco Bay, and shortly before Christmas, he took a trip to Miami, Florida, and stopped over for a brief visit in Cuba on his way to Puerto Rico. While the constant movement took his attention off of the political problems back home, the trips took him away from the ones he loved the most. Shortly before he took the trip to Florida and on to Puerto Rico, he wrote to Bess:

It was grand to talk with you and Margie. I'm so homesick I'm about to blow up and have been for two months. It is a miserable state of affairs when a man dreads showing up in his home town because all his friends are either in jail or about to go there. But that has been my state of mind ever since the special session. The Star and even Willie [William Randolph Hearst] *never fail to emphasize my friendships with people whom they think may be a detriment politically to me. Maybe I'm getting thin-skinned or something. Anyway I've got no business writing you about it.*[109]

Harry had been so busy that he had not declared that he was a candidate for reelection to the U.S. Senate. In fact, he was trying to decide what to do. In late January, he and some of his close supporters had a meeting at the Statler Hotel in St. Louis. During the meeting, Stephen Early, President Roosevelt's advisor, called Harry and offered him a lifetime appointment on the Interstate Commerce Commission. The position had an annual salary that exceeded his Senate salary of $10,000. Harry refused the offer, and Truman supporters held another meeting in Kansas City. At this meeting, which occurred one day before the filing deadline, he decided to seek reelection. It was clear that Franklin Roosevelt had some concerns about Harry Truman continuing as a senator from Missouri. What was also clear was that if Truman decided to seek reelection, he could no longer depend on the Pendergast machine to deliver votes because the machine was in shambles.[110]

The Trumans headed back to Washington in January 1940, and Bess and Margaret stayed in Washington until June 1940. Harry stayed busy with his Senate duties during this time, and he returned in July to begin his reelection campaign. He decided to move his statewide campaign headquarters to Sedalia, Missouri, which was located about sixty miles to the east of Kansas City. He wanted to move his campaign out of Kansas City to distance himself from the city. Sedalia was also a major railroad hub and had a significant union presence, and Harry made a strong appeal to organized labor in this contest.

Harry officially kicked off his Senate reelection campaign on June 15, 1940, in Sedalia, Missouri, in a daylong event that culminated with the junior senator delivering an evening speech to a packed square in Sedalia. His campaign outlined a plan that was strongly supportive of Franklin Roosevelt's New Deal, and he specifically appealed to farmers, union members, African Americans and women in his campaign. He knew that it would be a tough fight, and he campaigned harder than he ever had before. His campaign schedule was grueling—flying quickly to Washington to take care of his Senate business and then turning right around and catching a plane back to Missouri, where he hit the campaign trail.[111]

Harry's challengers in the August Senate primary included fellow Democrats Governor Lloyd Stark and Maurice Milligan. Both Stark and Milligan took credit for bringing down the Pendergast machine and made sure that voters were aware that Harry Truman was part of that machine. Voters went to the polls on August 6, and Harry prevailed, winning by only 7,976 votes.[112]

After the primary election win, Harry quickly returned to Washington. His colleagues enthusiastically embraced him, and he wrote back to Bess in Independence, describing the reception he received:

It certainly is gratifying (to put it mildly) when every employee in the building—elevator boys, policemen, waiters, cooks, negro cleanup women, and all—were interested in what would happen to me. [Les] *Biffle* [majority secretary of the Senate] *told me last night over the phone that no race in his stay here had created such universal interest in the Senate.*

He also described the election night that he spent with Margaret and Bess at home at 219 North Delaware:

I'll never forget Tuesday night if I live to be a thousand—which I won't. My sweet daughter and my sweetheart were in such misery it was torture to me. I wished then I'd never had made the fight. But it was a good fight: state employees—five or six thousand of them—the police departments of St. Louis, Kansas City, St. Joseph, and every election board in the state where there is one, all the big papers except the [Kansas City] *Journal, and those papers using every lie told on me as the truth. I hope some good fact-finder will make a record of that campaign. It will be history someday.*[113]

Harry Truman's August primary election win, without the support of the Pendergast machine, sent a strong message to Roosevelt that Harry was a legitimate political contender, and while Roosevelt did not enthusiastically endorse him, he did not try to thwart his election in November against the Republican candidate, Manvel Davis. Harry claimed one significant accomplishment as the campaign closed in on the November election. On September 18, 1940, Congress approved the Transportation Act of 1940, also known as the Truman Wheeler Transportation Act, which established new federal standards for American railroad, trucking and shipping industries. When the final votes were cast in November, Truman defeated Davis by 930,775 (51.2 percent) to 886,376 (48.7 percent.). He returned to Washington triumphant—elected on his own, with no ties to a political machine.[114]

When Harry returned to Washington in January 1941, the world was still wrapped up in the Second World War, and the United States had not joined the conflict as a combatant nation; however, the country was preparing for war and had been in earnest since the fall of France to Germany in June 1940. The U.S. Congress had increased military appropriations; however, Harry began hearing from his constituents in Missouri about waste in some of these government contracts.

In response to these concerns, and after checking out some of the situations on his own, Harry delivered a speech on February 10, 1941, before the U.S.

Senate that encouraged the Senate to create a committee to investigate the national defense program. He was concerned about cost overruns in the construction of camps and also that small business owners were being shut out of these defense contracts. He then introduced a resolution to establish a committee that would investigate the defense industry, and the resolution passed the Senate on March 1, 1941. The Senate created the Special Committee to Investigate the National Defense Program (known as the Truman Committee) and approved the expenditure of $15,000 to allow the committee to do its work. In mid-April 1941, the committee began its hearings, and the remainder of Truman's Senate career was spent working with the committee even after the United States declared war and entered World War II on December 8, 1941.[115]

On the day the Japanese bombed Pearl Harbor, December 7, 1941, Harry was in Columbia, Missouri, and he sent Bess a letter that described how his work on the committee had been received before he learned about the attack: "It's funny how things change around in thirteen months. I'm on the front pages of the *Kansas City Star*, *St. Louis Star-Times*, and *Kansas City Journal* for yesterday and am on the front page of the *Post-Dispatch* editorial section for today and mentioned in about three or four other places in the other parts of the paper and the *Globe*."[116]

Time magazine recognized Harry Truman and the work of the Truman Committee by placing him on the cover of the magazine in March 1943. As the Democratic convention rolled around in July 1944, Roosevelt was up for reelection to an unprecedented fourth term; however, there was a problem with his vice presidential candidate, Henry Wallace. Urban machine bosses and representatives from the labor unions wanted Wallace removed from the ticket, and they looked for a replacement. Before Harry left for the convention, Senator James Byrnes called him at his home and asked if he would support his candidacy for the vice presidency. Harry told him that he would. Almost as soon as Harry got off the phone with Byrnes, he received another phone call—this time from Senator Alben Barkley, who also asked Harry to support his candidacy for vice president. Harry told him that he had already committed to Byrnes and then made his way to Chicago for the convention.

After he arrived at the convention, he learned that some of the political bosses and union leaders wanted him to serve as the vice presidential nominee. Franklin Roosevelt even supported the decision. It was quite a turn of events from 1940, when Roosevelt had essentially written his political obituary, to July 1944, when Roosevelt asked Truman to serve as his running mate. His work on the defense committee had paid off. Bess and Margaret accompanied him to Chicago and were prominently featured as the convention selected Harry Truman to serve as Franklin Roosevelt's vice president.

On July 22, 1944, Madge Gates Wallace, who was staying with her son, Fred, in Denver, Colorado, wrote to Bess, "We are still excited but happy this morning after yesterday's thrill of Harry's nomination!"[117] Natalie Wallace told her sister-in-law, "Tell Harry for us that we are very proud of him and if it is what he wants we are for him." She also requested that she send a "secretary to answer the phone." In a prophetic line, Natalie told Bess that one woman who called told her that if Roosevelt died, Bess would "make a very gracious first lady."[118] Independence embraced his nomination as well. On July 23, 1944, the family returned to Independence, where they found that the Independence Chamber of Commerce had decorated the square with "Congratulations Senator Harry S. Truman" signs on the northwest and southeastern corners of the courthouse lawn. The Trumans spent the night at Frank and Natalie's house, and the next day, they greeted at least three thousand friends and supporters at an event held in their backyard.[119]

Harry voted in the August primary and then departed for Washington to attend to Senate business. He resigned his chairmanship of the Senate Investigative Committee and then, on August 18, attended a White House luncheon hosted by President Roosevelt. He described what happened next to Bess:

> *Then lunch was announced and we went out into the back yard of the White House under an oak tree planted by old Andy Jackson, and the movie men and then the flashlight boys went to work. He finally got hungry and ran 'em out. Then his daughter, Mrs Boettiger, acted as hostess and expressed a lot of regret that you were not there. I told the President that you were in Missouri attending to my business there, and he said that was O.K. He gave me a lot of hooey about what I could do to help the campaign and said he thought I ought to go home for an official notification and then go to Detroit for a labor speech and make no more engagements until we had had another conference. So that's what I'm going to do.*[120]

Since Roosevelt's health was failing, Harry did most of the campaigning in the fall after Labor Day. At 9:00 p.m. on November 3, 1944, Harry Truman's campaign train arrived at Union Station in Kansas City. Bess and Margaret departed from the train, and all three stayed at the Muehlebach Hotel in downtown Kansas City. The next day, the City of Independence sponsored a parade, and that evening, Truman delivered

The Presidential Electors of the United States
request the pleasure of the company of
Honorable Harry S. Truman and Mrs. Truman
as Guest of Honor
at the Inaugural Dinner in honor of
Franklin Delano Roosevelt
President of the United States
and
Harry S. Truman
Vice-President of the United States
Friday evening, January nineteenth
nineteen hundred and forty-five
at seven o'clock
The Mayflower
Washington

Committee on Arrangements
Robert E. Hannegan
Chairman National Democratic Committee
Honorary Chairman
Michael Francis Doyle
Chairman Electoral Colleges
Edwin A. Halsey
Secretary of the Senate
Homer S. Cummings
Treasurer

R.s.v.p.

The Trumans' 1944 inaugural invitation. *Truman Library.*

the final speech of the campaign at the RLDS Auditorium. Instead of
spending election eve, November 7, 1944, at home in Independence, the
family returned to the Muehlebach.[121]

Harry Truman was inaugurated as vice president of the United States
on January 20, 1945. Some Independence family members and residents

traveled to Washington for the festivities. Natalie Wallace was present for the ceremonies, and when she returned, she sent Bess a letter thanking her "for all you did for us." She then wrote, "I've decided you must like Independence or us very much to make the trip back and forth as often as you do."[122]

The Truman family moved back to Washington, and Harry assumed the duties of vice president. Bess continued her activities as the wife of the vice president, and Margaret attended George Washington University, where she received an Associate of Arts degree in 1944 and a Bachelor of Arts degree in history in 1946. She also launched a singing career after graduation and made her first outdoor appearance at the Hollywood Bowl on August 23, 1947. Mrs. D.W. Wallace accompanied her daughter and granddaughter to Washington.

President and First Lady, 1945–1953

I want you to know there [are] a great many of us who pray for our beloved President each night that he may enjoy good health and sail the ship of state on the right course, and we will welcome the day he may return to North Delaware St and be one of us.[123]

—*L.L. Compton, 318 North Delaware*

On April 12, 1945, Harry Truman sat down and dictated a letter to his sister-in-law, May Wallace, in Independence. He told her, "The situation back here gets no better fast. It looks as if I have more to do than ever and less time to do it, but some way we get it done. If I don't get this letter dictated to you, I will never get it written." In the afternoon, he presided over the Senate and then recessed the legislative body for the day before heading over to the House, where he had a drink with Sam Rayburn, the Speaker of the House. Rayburn told him that Stephen Early, Roosevelt's advisor, had phoned and wanted Harry to call back immediately. He put a call through to Early, who told him that he was needed at the White House. By the time he arrived at the White House, it was 5:30 p.m., and he went to the second floor, which was the family quarters. He met Mrs. Roosevelt, and she informed him that President Roosevelt had died at about 3:45 p.m. in Warm Springs, Georgia. Truman then went to the Oval Office, where he called Bess to tell her the news. Bess, who was accompanied by Margaret, arrived at the White House, and they assembled with Harry in the cabinet room, where Chief Justice

Harlan Stone administered the presidential oath of office at 7:09 p.m. that made Harry Truman president of the United States.[124]

Later that evening, or perhaps the next day, the letter that Harry Truman dictated earlier in the day on April 12 to his sister-in-law crossed his desk for his signature. In his own handwriting, Truman scrawled across the bottom of the letter, "This was dictated before the world fell in on me. But I've talked to you since and you know what a blow it was. But—I must meet it."[125]

The United States, and the world, had known no other president except Roosevelt since 1933. President Truman was under immense pressure because World War II still raged, and his immediate task was managing the war. The country and the world wondered who Harry Truman was and, more importantly, if he was up to the task.

News of President Roosevelt's death quickly reached Independence. What was interesting was the response his fellow family members, friends and neighbors had when they learned that Harry Truman was president. Natalie Wallace was concerned about Bess as she dashed off a letter:

> I wrote you a note Thursday night but between the phone, the radio, and being emotionally upset it was rather a mess so [I] tore it up. We are very proud of the honor that has come to Harry and are very confident that he can shoulder the burden and carry on. As for the "first lady" we know that she is quite capable of filling her place. There are lots of things that I would say if I were anything of a writer. So many times through the winter I have thought back to last summer and what a nice one it was. There seemed to be a feeling of unity in the Wallace family that had been lacking for some time and I was hoping that we might have such a summer this year.
>
> So many people have called and all expressed the same feeling of confidence in Harry. Mrs. Frank Jennings called for her mother, Mrs. Yingling. She has a broken hip but as soon as she heard the word said that she must get right up and write Harry. Wanted to express her confidence in him. Said Harry was one of her boys.[126]

Nellie and Ethel Noland, who were teaching at schools in the Kansas City area but still living across the street at 216 North Delaware, learned of President Roosevelt's death after they had visited a friend at a local hospital. Nellie Noland recalled that her first reaction was, "Harry is President and we didn't want him to be. It is a terrible responsibility to place on any man, and we couldn't help but feel sorry that this had to happen. Harry is so conscientious and such a hard worker and we know he will do a good job."

Ethel remembered that her first reaction was, "Poor Harry! It is such a hard job, but Harry can do it if anyone can. I hope everyone will be sympathetic because Harry will need the support of all for the tasks ahead. We still just can't realize that he is President."[127]

The Noland home had a picture window that looked right out on North Delaware Street and 219 North Delaware. For the next seven years, they watched the Truman family come and go, and they witnessed the crowds that surrounded the home—in many instances right up to the front door. In October 1949, they watched the construction of a fence that surrounded 219 North Delaware to prevent people from crowding so close to the doorway. Nellie Noland told Harry, "The White House yard is surrounded now by iron fence posts…The cars from everywhere continue to stop and pictures of all sorts of groups are taken. If I had time and skill, I would like to describe the cross-section of America that we see here on North Delaware every day."

The Nolands had a unique spot to view history, and Mary Ethel Noland had a unique role during the presidency in that she kept track of the Truman genealogy for the president, and she frequently responded to individuals who claimed to be related to the Truman family. The cousins frequently exchanged letters with their famous cousin and on several occasions, when

Workers install the iron fence around the Truman home in October 1949. *Truman Library.*

the family was away, lamented the fact that the lights were not burning at 219 North Delaware.[128]

Mayor Roger Sermon, who had served as Independence's mayor since 1924, told a *Kansas City Times* reporter:

> *The people of the United States can be assured that our nation will be safe under the leadership of Harry Truman.*
>
> *Harry Truman has been a deep student of politics and government for many years. His service in the United States Senate has given him a broad experience in international affairs and has equipped him to assume the duties ahead…I'm sure he will direct this nation safely through the critical years ahead.*[129]

George Dodsworth, president of the Independence Chamber of Commerce, sent the president a telegram that read:

> *We share with you the shock and sorrow of the sudden death of President Roosevelt, but hasten to assure you of our confidence in your leadership of the nation at this critical period. The citizens of your home community, who know you best, are trusting in your judgment and ability.*[130]

Harry responded to Dodsworth, as he did to many of his family, friends and neighbors who sent him notes of encouragement:

> *It is a source of pride to have my friends of the old home community stand behind me now with such assurances of confidence and with their prayers. I want all of you to know what a help it was to receive the kind message you sent me in their behalf through the Chamber of Commerce.*[131]

Both Harry and Bess Truman had established an extensive network of family and friends throughout their years in Independence. Bess's main support group included her Bridge Club. Bridge Club members included Helena Crow, Edna Hutchison, Linda King, Maggie Noel, Thelma Pallette, Lucy Peters, Mary Shaw, Adelaide Twyman, Natalie Wallace and May Wallace. The Bridge Club's visit to Washington in 1946 generated much favorable press and created a lifetime of memories for every Bridge Club member who made the trip. Harry also had a number of networks, including political, Masonic and military associates; however, if he wanted to spend some time with a few close associates in Independence, he usually spent

Bess Truman and Margaret Truman pose for a group photo with members of Bess Truman's Independence, Missouri bridge club outside the White House. *Left to right:* Mary Shaw, Adelaide Twyman, Natalie Wallace, Lucy Peters, Margaret Truman, Anne Peters Boyle, May Wallace, Helena Crow, Bess Truman, Thelma Pallette, Mag B. Noel, Edna Hutchison and Linda King, April 11, 1946. *Truman Library.*

time with the Harpie Club. Harpie Club members included the postmaster of Independence, Edgar "Hinie" Hinde; Polly Compton; W.F. "Bill" Lewis; Dexter Perry; and Mayor Roger Sermon, just to name a few.

The mayor waited until everything had settled down in Washington before he drafted a letter to President Truman in May 1945. By then, the national press had descended on the community to uncover just who Harry Truman was. Mayor Sermon, who owned a grocery store on the square, described the situation:

> *I have been radioed, photo*[graphed]*, and interviewed so much in the past month that even I began to feel important. You surely put the place on the map. The photographers have insisted on taking my picture, or rather the picture of your home town mayor in his store coat to give it the common touch and to prove that at one time you associated with vulgar tradesmen. Of course I am always brought back to earth the next morning when the*

alarm goes off at six. I have been rather amused at some of the reporters who have come out of the East. It seems that they had expected to find curiosities and strange looking creatures walking the streets. I have had a lot of fun with them and invite them to go up to the Square and I will show them the Indians and gypsies.

Sermon praised Harry for selecting Charlie Ross to serve as his press secretary. Ross graduated first in the same high school class as Harry in 1901 and went on to have a successful newspaper career, serving as the contributing editor of the *St. Louis Post Dispatch* before Harry tapped him to be his press secretary. Both Ross and Truman were well-known students of Ardelia Hardin Palmer and Tillie Brown.

Toward the end of April 1945, neighbor Henry Bundschu, who lived at 601 West Maple and whose family owned Bundschu's Department Store, which was located on the Independence Square, fired off a letter to his fellow neighbor after he learned that "Independence is going to be the summer Capital." Bundschu told Harry, "You could search the world over and not find a better place—and I don't mean maybe! I have been after Frank [Wallace] to get the house painted. He and George [Wallace] are talking about it. I think it should be white." In May, he updated the president on work in the neighborhood. "Your neighbors and friends are busy painting their houses and cleaning up their yards so that the neighborhood will look nice when you and Bess come to spend the summer." Bundschu was the first neighbor to write a biographical sketch of the president, titled "Harry S. Truman: The Missourian," which was published in the December 26, 1948 Sunday edition of the *Kansas City Star*.[132]

In May, the community breathed a sigh of relief when Germany surrendered on May 8, 1945. May 8 was Harry Truman's birthday, and he was relieved that the war in Europe had come to the end; however, in Asia, the war continued. Back home in Independence, work continued at the Summer White House on the grounds and on the home.

In June 1945, a local newspaper article reported that Harrison Irving, an African American man who served as the Trumans' "yardman" for the last eight years, was working in the yard. He told the reporter that Mrs. Truman was "mighty particular about the yard, and she's partial to peonies." He took the reporter to the back of the house, where the rose arbor was located and where deep red, pink and white peonies were in full bloom along the driveway. Harrison told the reporter that President Truman liked roses of all colors but then shared that "the deep red ones are his favorites."[133]

On June 3, 1945, Frank, Natalie, George and May greeted Bess, Margaret and Mrs. Wallace as they arrived at what now came to be known as the Summer White House. Before her arrival, Orville Campbell had overseen the painting of the home. After Bess arrived, she had to pick out new wallpaper patterns. She also interviewed Vietta Garr, the African American woman who had served as a domestic worker for the family from 1928, when Madge Gates Wallace hired her to work in the home, until 1943, when she left the Trumans to manage the Crown drugstore lunch counter. Bess wanted to know if Vietta would be interested in working at 219 North Delaware during the summer months, and she agreed to come back.[134]

Vietta Garr, resident of 131 East Farmer, was born Ione Vietta Garr in March 1896 to Benjamin and Emma Garr. Benjamin was born in 1858 into slavery on a farm that was located near Independence. After the Civil War, the family farmed around Independence and became active in the Baptist church. Some evidence suggests that Benjamin became a houseman for George Porterfield Gates, the father of Madge Gates Wallace, and that he also took care of horses or mules and served as a laborer at a local rock quarry. Vietta's mother, Emma, served as a laundress.

While Bess wanted Vietta to do most of the cooking, after 1945, she specifically wanted her to help take care of Bess's mother. According to the National Park Service, "Vietta knew what foods each of the Trumans enjoyed. During their stays in Independence, she fixed steam-fried chicken or baked Virginia ham, her own special recipe for sweet potatoes and the President's favorite, angel food cake." Vietta also assisted Bess in taking care of their daughter, Margaret. When Margaret launched a singing career, Vietta, whom Margaret often referred to as "Petey," often accompanied her on her concert tours.

When not working for the Trumans, Vietta was active in the Second Baptist Church. She often prepared food for church functions, played the piano and sang soprano in the church choir. She was also an active member in the Order of Twelve of the Knights and Daughters of Tabor. The organization was formed in 1872 and had as its objectives spreading Christianity and education, as well as acquiring real estate and supporting temperance.[135]

Leola Estes, another African American woman, also worked for the Trumans during the senatorial, presidential and post-presidential years. She split time working for the Trumans and the Allen family, who were located close to the Truman home. Barbara Allen remembered Vietta and Leola, noting, "Oh, there's no way you could not love Vietta or Leola. You're talking about very wonderful women. Very wonderful women. Loving, kind,

Vietta Garr (left) and Leola Estes arrive for Margaret Truman's wedding at the Trinity Episcopal Church, April 21, 1956. *Truman Library.*

gracious, patient." Of Vietta, she specifically recalled, "Unending source of lemonade and peanut and butter and jelly sandwiches. A wonderful cook, a lovely lady."[136]

The Trumans settled in, and Bess continued to oversee the remodeling of the Summer White House. On June 14, the *Independence Examiner* announced that Harry Truman would join his family for his first visit to his hometown as president on June 27, 1945. The very next day, Bob Snyder, at 414 North Lexington, who was foreman of the five-man crew that was painting the fourteen-room Victorian Summer White House, reported that his crew would complete the painting project in about a week. The Noland home, across the street, also sported a new paint job, and Ethel and Nellie were busy cleaning their home. Further down Delaware, Miss Ruth Cook, at 610 North Delaware, daughter of Mr. and Mrs. Louis Cook, was not sure whether she would be able to mow the lawn in time for the president's arrival.[137]

The Independence Police Department also prepared for the president's arrival. Chief of Police Hal Phillips and his force of fourteen officers were supplemented by a force of twenty-five auxiliary policemen. Phillips told a reporter that "[o]ur men know who should be allowed in the neighborhood" and that "we are prepared to handle any traffic situation."[138]

The Independence Chamber of Commerce erected more than two thousand banners that read, "Welcome Home, Mr. President" on businesses and residences that surrounded the square. The chamber spent almost $3,500 to purchase flags and light fixtures that were placed on the square; however, chamber president George Dodsworth said that those would not be in place for Truman's first visit. Dodsworth also said that eleven road signs that proclaimed Independence, Missouri, as the home of Harry Truman would be placed along U.S. Highway 40 and 24 and on Highway 71. In January 1945, the chamber placed a sign at the intersection of Highway 24 and Noland Road that proclaimed, "Home of Vice-President Harry S. Truman." That sign was changed to read, "Home of President, Harry S. Truman."[139] On June 25, 1945, Mayor Roger Sermon presented a flagpole

Mayor Roger Sermon presented a flagpole to the Truman family in 1945 for the Summer White House. When the flag was flown, it meant that the family was at home. *Truman Library.*

to the Truman family that was erected on the front lawn. If the flag was flying atop the pole, it meant that the family was home.

The president's airplane touched down at the Fairfax Airport in Kansas City, Kansas, on the afternoon of June 27, 1945. The touchdown marked the first time that Harry Truman had visited his hometown as president, and his friends and neighbors were ready. Margaret met him at the airport along with a throng of others. He got in a blue Cadillac convertible donated by J.E. (Honey) Latimer of Latimer Motors for the fifteen-mile journey home. All along the route, crowds gathered to greet him, and he enthusiastically waved back to them. As the procession entered Independence, the blue Cadillac made its way to the Independence Square, where he found well-wishers everywhere and the square decked out in the decorations that the Independence Chamber of Commerce had provided. His entourage proceeded down West Maple Avenue in front of the Memorial Building, the president's polling place, which was also decorated for the occasion. The car then turned on to North Delaware and finally arrived at his home.

A crowd had gathered in front of the home to greet him. At the time, the home did not have a fence, so all of the people crowded onto the lawn of

Harry Truman riding in a blue Cadillac convertible on his first visit to Independence as president, June 27, 1945. *Truman Library.*

219 North Delaware and right up to the front door. The president settled in for a few minutes, but he had a busy afternoon and evening planned.[140]

At 3:50 p.m., the president came out of 219 North Delaware and walked two blocks to the Memorial Building, where he presided over a press conference—the first and only official press conference he held in the city during his tenure as president. Members of the press descended on the building and were waiting when he arrived. Just before his arrival, Harry was in San Francisco, where he signed the United Nations (UN) charter. At the press conference, he encouraged the Senate to ratify the charter and told those assembled that it was "necessary to the future of America and the world that the words of the Charter be built into the solid structure of peace for which the world is waiting and praying." He also announced at the press conference that he accepted the resignation of Secretary of State Edward Stettinius Jr. and appointed him as the representative of the United States to the United Nations.

The press asked the president questions, and one member asked if he would say a few words about his homecoming reception. He responded, "I was overwhelmed with it, of course. All these people have seen me two or three times a day, for the last 30 or 40 years. I can't see what there is about me now that would make them turn out like they did today." One member of the local press who attended the press conference was Sue Gentry, who lived at 722 West Waldo. Colonel William Southern, owner of the *Independence Examiner*, had tapped her to be the city editor in 1943, and she remained city editor until 1953; however, she continued to cover President Truman and his family in the post-presidential years until 1973, when she retired.[141]

Truman walked back to his home from the press conference and then headed to Grandview, Missouri, to visit his mother. The visit was short because he soon returned to Independence, and at 6:15 p.m., he headed to the home of Mayor Roger Sermon, at 701 Proctor Place, for a reception held in his honor. A throng of people assembled on the lawn in front of the home and greeted him before he entered Sermon's home at 7:00 p.m. He left at 7:45 p.m. to attend a homecoming program planned in his honor at the RLDS Auditorium.

Mayor Sermon introduced the president:

> *It is not necessary for me to tell you that we are glad to have you back. This great crowd of neighbors and friends is abundant evidence of that…*
>
> *We hope the time never comes when you are tired and discouraged and everything seems to go wrong, but if it does, just come back to us. We will understand and a hearty hand shake and a pat on the back will be ready.*

The president rose to speak and told the crowd of ten thousand that there were two important things that he needed to accomplish as president. "The first one is to win the war with Japan, and we are winning it. The next is to win the peace."[142]

The next day, Harry Truman popped out of 219 North Delaware at 9:00 a.m. and went across the street to visit his cousins and aunt, Mrs. J.T. Noland, sister of his late father, John A. Truman. After about a ten-minute visit, he headed to Kansas City, where he went to his office at the Federal Building. The president departed Independence for Washington on June 30, 1945.[143]

The president had a busy schedule in Washington after the first visit. In July, he traveled to Potsdam, Germany, where he conferred with representatives from the Soviet Union and Great Britain on war aims. They decided to focus their efforts on Japan. It was at Potsdam that Truman received news that a nuclear bomb test in the desert of New Mexico was successful. On August 6 and August 9, the United States dropped atomic bombs on the Japanese cities of Hiroshima and Nagasaki, and on August 14, 1945, the Japanese surrendered. World War II officially ended; however, much work remained, including how the American economy would retool from a wartime to a peacetime economy and what role the United States would play in world affairs as a Cold War developed between the United States and the Soviet Union.

On September 15, 1945, Harry and Bess Truman arrived at the Kansas City Municipal airport at about 7:00 p.m. They were greeted by Margaret at the airport, along with the president's sister and brother, Mary Jane and Vivian. The couple, along with other family members and their Secret Service detail, got into a black limousine for the trip to 219 North Delaware, where they found two hundred well-wishers to greet them. The president quickly went inside, and his friend Fred A. Canfil encouraged the crowd to disperse, which it did; however, the president came back out around 7:50 p.m. with Margaret, and the pair headed across the street to the Nolands. Truman carried a framed photograph of himself for his aunt and a gold-trimmed box that contained three bottles of French perfume that he purchased for Nellie and Ethel on his trip to Germany.

On Sunday morning, a small crowd gathered in front of the home at about 9:00 a.m., and Harry greeted the visitors. Most of those who assembled were his immediate neighbors. Eighty-seven-year-old Rees Alexander, at 814 West Van Horn (now Truman Road), rushed over to shake his hand. Rees told the president that he had voted in seventeen elections and that in his first election he voted for Hancock. Harry told him, "That was four years before I was born." L.L. "Polly" Compton, owner of Polly's Pop, was present, and when the president told the crowd that he decided to stay home from church that morning and read what the papers were saying about him instead because he thought his presence might create quite a stir at the church service, Compton told the president that the newspapers were saying "nice" things about him. Truman recognized another neighbor in the crowd, John J. Major, of 220 North Delaware, and told him that he was glad to see him. Major responded, "We're glad to have you home, too." He then told him, "We just want you to know we're all for you." Harry responded, "I want to thank you because I need all the help I can get."[144]

On September 16, 1945, Harry returned to Washington by himself, and Bess, Margaret, Madge and Vietta returned two weeks later. The family remained in Washington and did not return to 219 North Delaware until the holidays in December. Bess, Margaret, Madge and Vietta were scheduled to arrive back in Independence via train on the evening of December 19; however, mechanical difficulties delayed their arrival until the early morning hours of December 20. As was the custom, George, May, Frank and Natalie greeted the family when they arrived.[145]

When the family arrived at home, the Independence Chamber of Commerce had already shoveled the sidewalks clean of one foot of snow in front of 219 North Delaware. The sixteen-foot Douglas fir, compliments of Marion and David Wallace, Fred and Christine's children, sat in the backyard in a crate, awaiting its placement and decoration in the front bay windows of 219 North Delaware by Margaret Truman.

The only person who was not present was Harry Truman. His work as president detained him; however, in preparation for the holiday, he received some correspondence from his friends and neighbors. On December 15, 1945, Ernest L. Capps, who specialized in raising broad-breasted bronze turkeys in Liberty, Missouri, sent Harry a telegram asking him when Mrs. Truman wanted him to send a turkey to 219 North Delaware for Christmas. He replied December 24. On December 18, 1945, Mize Peters, of 631 North Delaware, sent Truman a letter asking him whether he and his family would be able to continue the tradition of dropping by their house Christmas evening, as they had done before Harry became president. Truman quickly dashed off a letter to Peters, saying, "I am looking forward to seeing you during Christmas week."[146]

Ernest Capps's son, Jack, whom Truman had appointed to go to West Point, delivered the turkey on December 24. Unfortunately, the weather detained Harry in Washington, and he did not arrive until Christmas Day.

The Truman family spent every Christmas at 219 North Delaware except the Christmas of 1947, the year Harry's mother died, and the Christmas of 1952, the year Bess's mother passed away. For the 1948, 1949 and 1951 Christmases, Truman delivered the address to light the National Community Christmas tree on Christmas Eve from his home in Independence. In 1950, he lit the National Christmas tree from 219 North Delaware; however, Harry delivered a prerecorded address.

Harry Truman lighting the National Community Christmas Tree in Washington, D.C., from his home at 219 North Delaware, December 24, 1951. Photograph by Vernon Galloway. Truman Library.

The 1948 Christmas address was probably the most memorable:

> *I have come out here to Independence with my family to celebrate the great home festival. For of all the days of the year Christmas is the family day. Christmas began that way…*
>
> *There are no ties like family ties. That is why I have made the journey back to Independence to celebrate this Christmas Day among the familiar scenes and associations of my old hometown…*
>
> *This country, big as it has grown, has always been a close-knit community. It has to be strong, too. We needed the strength of giants and heroic courage to bring nature and elements under control; to build our towns—and that is particularly true here in Independence—and extend our frontiers. We all know what the covered wagon symbolized…*
>
> *I have been thinking of all these things here in my home on North Delaware Street in Independence. I am speaking to you from our family living room. As I*

came up the street in the gathering dusk, I saw a hundred commonplace things that are hallowed to me on this Christmas Eve—hallowed because of their associations with the sanctuary of home.

I saw the lighted windows in the homes of my neighbors, the gaily decked Christmas trees, and the friendly lawns and gardens. The branches of the trees were bare and stark but somehow they looked familiar and friendly. I looked at all these familiar things—the same things that you all will see tonight as you go toward home…

I wish all of you a Merry Christmas.[147]

While Harry Truman made every effort to return to Independence for the Christmas holiday, he also made every effort to return to vote in primary and general elections. The most important election in which he returned home to vote was in the November 1948 general election.

On the morning of November 1, 1948, Harry Truman's Missouri Pacific train pulled into the Independence depot. About four hundred people gathered to greet him. He had to have been exhausted from campaigning almost nonstop for the last two months since he accepted the Democratic nomination for president at the Democratic convention in Philadelphia on July 15, 1948; however, coming home always gave him a lift. He told the crowd, "It's grand to be home. I can't tell you how much I appreciate your coming down to see the country boy come back to his home town. I've been through a terrific campaign, trying to convince the people that I'm doing what's right. When I see this big crowd here to greet me, I'm sure of it."[148]

Later that evening, from the comfort of 219 North Delaware, he delivered the final speech of the campaign. Across the street at 220 North Delaware, at the home of neighbors Mr. and Mrs. John Major, the National Broadcasting Company set up its operation to cover the speech. The American Broadcasting Company set up at the home of Mr. and Mrs. John Luff, 224 North Delaware. Other networks used the homes of Nellie and Ethel Noland and Miss Mary O'Reilly, at 218 North Delaware, as their base of operations during President Truman's visit.[149]

In his speech, which was broadcast nationwide, he told all Americans:

Tonight I am at my home here in Independence—Independence, MO.—with Mrs. Truman and Margaret. We are here to vote tomorrow as citizens of this Republic. I hope that all of you who are entitled to vote will exercise that great privilege. When you vote, you are in control of your Government.

Tomorrow you will be deciding between the principles of the Democratic Party—the party of the people—and the principles of the Republican Party—the party of privilege.

Your vote tomorrow is not just a vote for one man or another; it is a vote which will affect you and your families for years to come.[150]

The next day, Harry Truman started his day at 8:20 a.m. with a morning walk through the neighborhood. Then, around 10:00 a.m., Harry, Bess and Margaret Truman went to the Memorial Building to cast their ballots. This was the last time his name appeared on a ballot and the first time his mother, Martha Ellen Truman, was not able to see him vote—she passed away in 1947.

After voting, the president traveled to Grandview to visit his sister and brother and then, at 1:00 p.m., traveled to Rockwood Country Club for a luncheon. He returned home in the evening but then snuck out—under the watchful eye of the press and well-wishers who camped out in front of 219 North Delaware awaiting the election returns—to go to Excelsior

Harry Truman walking with Rufus Burrus on the Independence Square, December 27, 1949. *Truman Library.*

Harry Truman voting in the Memorial Building on November 2, 1948. *Truman Library.*

Springs, Missouri, to spend the night at the Elms Hotel alone, leaving Bess and Margaret to listen to the returns at home. He ate at 6:30 p.m. and then went to sleep; however, he got up at midnight to hear some of the returns, which had him behind in the polls. He went back to sleep, but at about 4:00 a.m., Secret Service agent Jim Rowley woke him up and encouraged him to listen to the returns on the radio—they described how Truman had pulled ahead in the polls over his Republican challenger, Thomas Dewey, by 2 million votes. He told his Secret Service detail to make preparations to return to Kansas City and the Muehlebach Hotel, where he maintained a private suite. He arrived at the suite at 6:00 a.m., and at 10:14 a.m., Dewey conceded the election.[151]

When word spread to Independence that he had won reelection, Mayor Roger Sermon proclaimed a city holiday, and the William Chrisman High School band made its way to 219 North Delaware to serenade the president. Margaret came out on the porch and thanked them for coming but told them that her father was not home and would not return until the afternoon. Meanwhile, city leaders organized an afternoon parade that traveled through the Independence Square and past the courthouse where Truman served as county judge.

President Truman finally arrived in Independence from Kansas City a little before 7:00 p.m. News spread that he would address the "home folk" on the steps of the courthouse, where he received his political start. He arrived on the south side of the courthouse steps at 7:45 p.m. to a packed square. In a short three-minute speech, he told those gathered:

The parade that erupted on the square in November 1948 (on Lexington Avenue) after the residents of the community learned that Harry Truman had won the presidency. *Truman Library.*

I can't tell you how very much I appreciate this turnout to celebrate a victory—not my victory, but a victory of the Democratic Party for the people...

And I think you very much indeed for this celebration, which is not for me. It is for the whole country. It is for the whole world, for the simple reason that you have given me a tremendous responsibility.

Now, since you have given me that responsibility, I want every single one of you to help carry out that responsibility, for the welfare of this great Republic, and for the welfare and peace of the world at large.

Truman delivered the speech before a crowd that included his former teachers, Battery D members, fellow Masons, political associates and his family members; they had supported him throughout his entire political career, which he described as all the way from the precinct to the presidency.[152]

Upon his election victory, neighbor Ray Wills, who owned a garage at 800 West Maple, attended the speech on the square, and he told the president in a letter, "My family and I joined the crowds that Wednesday night to pay homage to you." Earlier in the year, Wills, whose station was on Harry's walking route, had a heart attack and was hospitalized. When Harry learned

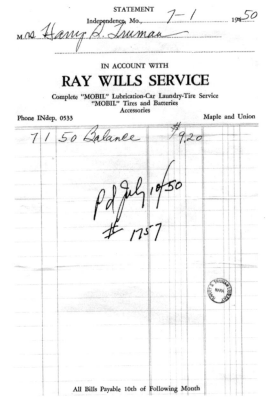

Ray Wills's garage, at Union and Maple Streets, serviced the Truman family vehicles. *Truman Library.*

of his hospitalization, he sent him a letter of encouragement that read, "Take good care of yourself, Union Street and Maple Avenue will not be the same corner unless you are there to make it run." Another neighbor, Luke Choplin, of 304 North Delaware, sent the president a congratulatory telegram: "We couldn't have been more thrilled if it had been a member of the family." He signed it, "Your friend and neighbor." Truman responded several weeks later, summing up his thoughts about his hometown support: "Many, many thanks for that fine telegram. Such thoughtful messages from old friends and neighbors mean more to me than I can say."[153]

John and Edna Hutchison, of 1121 South Main Street, also commented on the president's victory. John was a member of Harry's Harpie Club, and Edna was a member of Bess's Tuesday Bridge Club. Edna, who wrote the letter, told Truman, "I'm sure Mr. Dewey is relegated to knitting by the fireside for keeps by now. Johnny, a man of few words and no loose statements, says to tell you that he knows you are the greatest politician who ever lived." Harry responded with a letter of thanks of his own, and in his own handwriting at the bottom of the letter, he wrote, "I don't deserve such good opinions as yours and John's. But when home folks are like that it's all worth while!"[154]

In December 1948, the family returned home for the Christmas holiday. It was on this visit that Harry created the "Truman Walking Club" to honor those reporters who were fit enough to keep up with him on his morning walks. The Truman family attended a reception hosted by Charles A. Davis and his son, Blevins Davis, at Glendale, located just off Lee's Summit Road

Ray Wills (left) speaks with Harry Truman on one of his walks in front of 800 West Maple. *Truman Library.*

in Independence. The *Examiner* reported, "There were about 20 guests from K.C. from among those many of whom formerly lived in Independence and…a hundred home town friends."[155]

As the holidays wound down, family members, including the Wallaces and the Nolands, and other friends made plans to attend the January 20, 1949

The Truman Early Risers Walking Society of Independence, Mo. DEC. 22-29, 1948

The Truman Early Risers Club, December 1948. *Truman Library.*

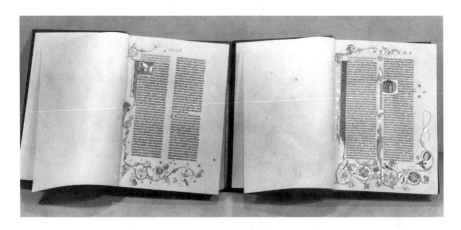

Residents of Independence and the chamber of commerce raised money to purchase this replica of a Gutenberg Bible that Harry Truman used in the 1949 inauguration. *Truman Library.*

inauguration. The Independence Chamber of Commerce and residents of Independence raised money and purchased a replica of the Gutenberg Bible that Harry used for his inaugural swearing-in ceremony. Delaware Street neighbor Mize Peters and Frank Rucker of the *Independence Examiner*, who represented the Independence Chamber of Commerce, coordinated the delivery of the Bible to Washington for the inauguration. The replica Gutenberg Bible and the Bible that Harry used when he was sworn in on the day of Roosevelt's death were used in the inauguration ceremony—the Gutenberg Bible was open to Exodus 20 and the other Bible to Matthew 5. When Truman was sworn in, he placed his left hand on the twentieth chapter of Exodus. Truman inscribed the Bible and returned it to Independence, where it was displayed at the Jackson County Library. Also, on inauguration day, Van Horn Road, the main east–west street that ran in front of 219 North Delaware, was renamed Truman Road.[156]

The Truman family continued to travel back and forth from Washington, D.C., to Independence in 1949. The next year, 1950, was a pivotal year in the life of Independence, the country and the world. Personally, for Harry Truman, it was a very challenging year. In January 1950, Mayor Roger Sermon died of a heart attack on the steps of the Independence City Hall. One of his favorite teachers, Matilda "Tillie" Brown, of 720 South Main, passed away in February 1950. Truman sent Tillie Brown's husband a thoughtful telegram:

> *I feel a deep sense of personal loss in the death of Miss Tillie. She was beloved by the thousands who had the rare privilege of attending her classes. "Great" is a word to be used sparingly, but I have no hesitancy in calling*

Dedication of the Liberty Bell at the Memorial Building, November 6, 1950. In 1959, the Liberty Bell was moved to the grounds of the Truman Library. *Photograph by Vernon Galloway. Truman Library.*

her a truly great teacher and a great woman. I owe a debt of gratitude to her and to her memory that can never be repaid.[157]

The crushing blow came on December 5, 1950, when Charlie Ross, his press secretary and fellow high school classmate, died of a heart attack. In addition to these deaths, the Cold War, which began as soon as the victory of the Second World War wore off, grew warmer as the Korean War commenced.

In June 1950, Harry Truman was home in Independence celebrating his thirty-first wedding anniversary when Secretary of State Dean Acheson called and informed him that North Korea had invaded South Korea. He quickly returned to Washington to plan a response, and the United States, fighting under the United Nations, planned the strategy for what became known as the Korean War. In November 1950, he returned to Independence to deliver a speech that marked the dedication of the placement of a replica of the Liberty Bell at the Memorial Building that the city of Annecy, France (where the bell was made), had sent to the city.

Of all of the speeches Truman delivered in Independence during his presidency, the one he gave at the Memorial Building on the afternoon of November 6, 1950, was the most important. Situated on the south side of the Memorial Building steps, in front of the entrance he usually used to enter the building to vote, Truman connected his personal history and the history of his community with the role he thought the United States needed to play in the Cold War:

> This is a great, great day for Independence. You know, I went to Sunday School right across there—the first time in my life, a long, long time ago, and in that Sunday School class I met a little, blue-eyed golden-haired girl—my first sweetheart. Her eyes are still blue, but her hair is no longer golden, it's silver—like mine. And she is still my sweetheart.
>
> I was graduated from high school right here on this corner, and the motto of that high school was "Youth, The Hope of the World."
>
> Youth are still the hope of the world, and will always be.
>
> This bell comes to the people of Independence as a gift from the people of Annecy, France. Annecy is a city in eastern France, near the Alps. It is not far from the Vosges mountains, where the 129th Field Artillery—in which I had the honor of serving—fought in the first World War, and where a good many American boys fought in the second world war. In both those wars, the people of the United States and the people of France fought on the same side—on the side of freedom and liberty…
>
> Today, the nations and peoples who believe in freedom face a bitter enemy. We are confronted by communist imperialism—a reactionary movement that despises liberty and is the mortal foe of personal freedom. The threat of communist aggression is a continuing menace to world peace…
>
> Our objective is to achieve a peace based on agreement among nations. And this is what the United Nations is working for.
>
> The United States stands today, and always has stood, for the settlement of differences among nations by peaceful means. I am convinced that most of the nations and other countries in the world stand for that same thing.
>
> But there are some nations in the world who will not have it that way. The leaders of Communist imperialism have chosen to follow the path of aggression. Through threats and through the use of force, they are seeking to impose their will upon peoples all over the world…
>
> Korea is proof that freedom can survive if the peoples who cherish it stand together. The common victory against aggression in Korea is evidence

that the free nations will not let communist imperialism swallow up the free peoples one by one...

Freedom has never been an abstract idea to us here in the United States. It is real and concrete. It means not only political and civil rights; it means much more. It means a society in which man has a fair chance. It means an opportunity to do useful work. It means the right to an education. It means protection against economic hazards...

Written around the crown of this bell are the words, "Proclaim liberty throughout the land and to all the inhabitants thereof." Those words are 2,500 years old. I learned the first line over there in that Presbyterian church. They come from the Bible. They reflect a deep belief in freedom under God and justice among men—a belief which is at the heart of what the Bible teaches us.

Our concept of freedom has deep religious roots. We come under a divine command to be concerned about the welfare of our neighbors, and to help one another. For all men are the servants of God, and no one has the right to mistreat his fellow men...

The fellowship of freedom is growing. It stands firm against the false prophets of Communism, who represent not brotherhood, but dictatorship—not progress, but reaction.

The fellowship of freedom will prevail against tyranny, and bring peace and justice to the world. For freedom is the true destiny of man.[158]

Harry's Latin teacher, Ardelia Hardin Palmer, of 406 North Pleasant, who attended a luncheon for the president before his speech but who was unable to get close enough to greet her former student, went home and watched her former pupil deliver the speech at the Memorial Building on television—it was broadcast to more than sixty countries. She told the president in a letter:

You "televise" fine! Your speech and tone were perfect—as was the setting. Memorial Hall, the Liberty Bell, the Statue of Liberty on the site of old Independence High School from which you graduated. You've always been, even from boyhood, the hope of our country—and now the whole world—the motto you quoted was symbolical. I wish Mr. Palmer had lived to see you President—the words "Juventus spes mundi" was his selection and he believed in you and your great destiny.[159]

The Latin inscription above the high school, *Juventus Spes Mundi*, was forever etched in the minds of its students. Nellie Noland, who graduated from Independence High School, invoked the phrase in a letter she sent to her cousin as she sat in front of the picture window at 216 North Delaware and watched the people file by the Summer White House in late October 1951:

> *Yesterday was Sunday and a perfect day. The trees in the yard at 219 were never so lovely before and such a crowd of admirers and picture-takers as there was in the street all day. It seemed to be such a representative middle-class crowd and nearly all of them young men and women and often their children. It reminded me of the motto that we all loved over our first high school—"Juventus spes Mundi." I am always interested in the crowds that are there and thrill to think that you are the attraction more than just the house.* [160]

In October 1951, the Korean War continued, and it did not go well. Truman fired General Douglas MacArthur, commander of UN and U.S. forces, for publicly disagreeing with the president over war strategy. By February 1952, Harry Truman was thinking about whether he would seek reelection. Cousin Ethel Noland wrote, "I know you are thoroughly enjoying the situation of the present time—keeping the world guessing as to what your intentions are…It's a good idea to keep them guessing." By April 1952, Truman had decided not to run. [161]

While Truman made his decision not to run, his mother-in-law, Madge Gates Wallace, lost her struggle with her health issues and died on December 5, 1952. The family returned to Independence on December 7, and Madge Gates Wallace's funeral was held at 219 North Delaware; however, the family did not stay for the Christmas holiday. It was the last visit the family would make to their hometown as president and first lady of the United States. Ethel Noland was sorry that Madge had passed away but also that they would not get to see the family at Christmas. She told the president, "Christmas has come and gone with nary a triple ring of the door bell. We missed it. It was the first time in a long time."

In the November election of 1952, Republican Dwight Eisenhower bested the Democratic candidate, Adlai Stevenson. On January 20, 1953, Harry and Bess attended the inauguration for the new president, and then they boarded a train bound for Independence. From December 6 to December 11, 1952, George Gallup conducted a poll that asked Americans whether they approved or disapproved of Harry Truman's job as president. The poll noted that his approval rating was 31 percent. [162]

Harry S Truman Historic District National Historic Landmark

Independence, Missouri

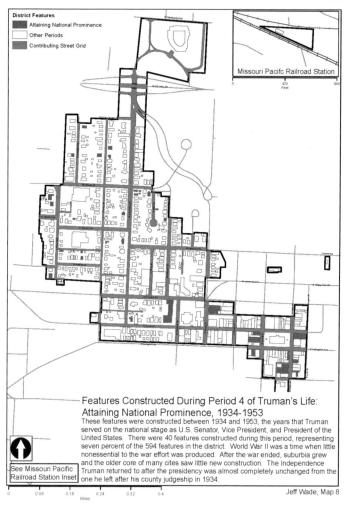

District Features

- Attaining National Prominence
- Other Periods
- Contributing Street Grid

Missouri Pacifc Railroad Station

0   420   840
Feet

Features Constructed During Period 4 of Truman's Life:
Attaining National Prominence, 1934-1953
These features were constructed between 1934 and 1953, the years that Truman served on the national stage as U.S. Senator, Vice President, and President of the United States. There were 40 features constructed during this period, representing seven percent of the 594 features in the district. World War II was a time when little nonessential to the war effort was produced. After the war ended, suburbia grew and the older core of many cites saw little new construction. The Independence Truman returned to after the presidency was almost completely unchanged from the one he left after his county judgeship in 1934.

See Missouri Pacific Railroad Station Inset

0   0.08   0.16   0.24   0.32   0.4
Miles

Jeff Wade, Map 8

Map by Jeff Wade.

While polls did not really matter to Harry, the fact that he was unable to bring the Korean War to a conclusion certainly had to have been on his mind as the train traveled west. There were other issues as well: his Cold War policies, the containment policy, the Marshall Plan and NATO. Were those the right policies? What about civil rights? He issued an executive

Harry S Truman Historic District National Historic Landmark
Independence, Missouri

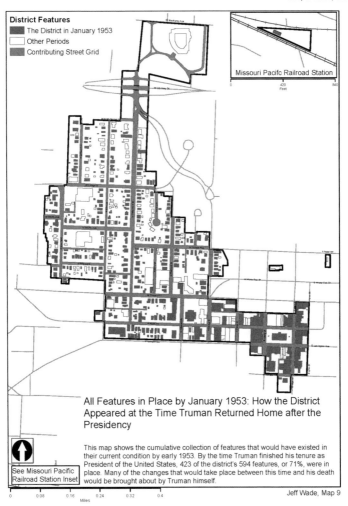

District Features
- The District in January 1953
- Other Periods
- Contributing Street Grid

Missouri Pacifc Railroad Station

All Features in Place by January 1953: How the District Appeared at the Time Truman Returned Home after the Presidency

This map shows the cumulative collection of features that would have existed in their current condition by early 1953. By the time Truman finished his tenure as President of the United States, 423 of the district's 594 features, or 71%, were in place. Many of the changes that would take place between this time and his death would be brought about by Truman himself.

See Missouri Pacific Railroad Station Inset

Jeff Wade, Map 9

Map by Jeff Wade.

order in 1948 that resulted in the integration of the military. How would all of those decisions pan out?

Surprisingly, when the ex-president arrived at Union Station in Washington to depart for Independence with Bess, he was met by a throng of supporters. As the train headed west, other people gathered along the way to greet him.

The presence of people along the route had to have buoyed his spirits. Later in life, he recalled, "They were there to see a fella who had served eight years in the White House leave town, which is not very usual. Well that happened all the way across the country from Washington until we got to Independence, Missouri, and it was heartwarming the way people acted."[163]

Returning to Independence, 1953-1982

Mrs. Truman and I decided to stay on Delaware Street in Independence, where we are quite comfortable.[164]

—*Harry S. Truman*

Late in the evening on January 21, 1953, the train pulled into the station at Independence, which still proudly displayed a large wooden sign that read, "Home of President Harry S. Truman." Truman was amazed that the "home folk" turned out to greet them. Mayor Robert Weatherford was one of the first to welcome him home, and he told the crowd gathered, "He'll always be Mr. President to us. He's home folks to us. We're glad to have him and we are glad to have all of you here to greet him tonight. Welcome home neighbor."

Harry responded:

> *Thank you very much Mr. Mayor. I can't tell you how very much Mrs. Truman and I appreciate this reception. It is magnificent. I never expected it therefore it is more to the heart than I anticipated that it would be. There is not much I can say to you except that your good feeling and thought of us is highly appreciated. We are back home now for good. I am in the army of the unemployed now—although it is a small army.*
>
> *I am here to tell you a little later on when I get the job done that Mrs. Truman has for me, which she says I am going to have to do is unpack all our goods and chattels—and it took about seven or eight men three months*

to get it done so I don't know how long it will take one man to get it undone. After that I will be open for dinner engagements and things of that kind because I might be hungry by that time. We do thank you immensely for this welcome. I don't see how anyone in the world could have a better one.

After the former president finished his remarks, someone in the crowd shouted, "We love you Harry." The couple then made their way to 219 North Delaware, where another crowd had gathered to welcome them home. The Nolands watched their homecoming from across the street.[165]

The community allowed Harry and Bess the opportunity to settle in, and then, on February 5, 1953, the community hosted an official homecoming event in their honor at the Laurel Club in the RLDS Auditorium. Blevins Davis—who directed the play that was put on to honor the 1933 remodeling of the Independence Courthouse, hosted the Truman family at Glendale during Christmas and, during Harry Truman's presidency, directed *Porgy and Bess*, which featured an interracial cast that toured Moscow—sent a letter from England, which was to be read at the homecoming celebration:

Tonight history is being written in Independence, Missouri, because the guest of honor is a great world-citizen, Harry S. Truman.

When any man shoulders the responsibility of the world and like an Atlas struggles to hold it high above the battle cry into the realm of Peace; to hold it against the destructive forces of insidious Communistic propaganda; to hold it above racial prejudice—then such a man is destined to walk a lonely path because many of his fellow men cannot act and think upon the same plane of accomplishment—nor lend him proper aid during his darkest hours. His <u>penalty</u> for such greatness comes when he realizes that all he has dreamed cannot be fulfilled in the short span of a life-time: his <u>reward</u> for his efforts and his greatness is <u>immortality</u>.

Here in England we feel and see the effects of his leadership. The same is true in Germany, Austria, France, Belgium, Italy, the turbulent Middle East, the seething Orient—all of these countries know this man is dedicated to the principles which can elevate humanity in a Free World. All continental Europe outside the iron curtain, the British people, and the entire English speaking union, pay tribute to our friend and fellow citizen because he saw to it that the United States brought hope to displace despair; gave food and shelter to the starving and homeless; entrenched Christianity again in the souls of men whose minds and hearts have been crushed by the disciples of death and destruction—Hitler, Mussolini, and Stalin.

Again I say, history is being written tonight in Independence. The "prophet" has returned, and not without honor, returned to his home and to his people who are thankful for what he has given to the age in which we live. People here, I assure you, pray for him and his family—for his well-being, and for his continued influence and leadership which is so badly needed in this troubled world.[166]

Mayor Weatherford then introduced the guest of honor:

Our love, our respect, and our admiration for this splendid family is here manifested, by your spontaneous outpouring for this homecoming reception honoring Mr. Truman, Mrs. Truman, and Miss Margaret Truman.

While Mr. Truman served this nation as the President of the United States, his every heartbeat had a purpose. His every thought visualized a service, and each prayer sought Divine guidance.

The truly great decisions of history rested themselves upon his shoulders and thereon balanced the future of unborn generations. With resolute faith and supreme courage, he faced the future, hand in hand with Almighty God, and the people of America.

We say to you, Mr. Truman, Mrs. Truman, and Miss Margaret, Missouri has cradled you, and you have done her honor. The people of the United States called you to their service. Your response to that call has brought to you the affection and gratitude of both free and enslaved peoples through the entire world.

And now, to you, a friendly welcome home, good neighbors and dear friends.

The former president then rose to speak:

Appreciation for this gathering, the one at the Washington Union Station, at stations along the way, through West Virginia, Ohio, Indiana and Illinois.

Wonderful reception at St. Louis, Washington, Missouri, Hermann, Jefferson City, Tipton. Then the climax of all the trip home at the R. R. depot in Independence, 9,000 or 10,000 friends and neighbors there, 5,000 at the front gate at 219 North Delaware.

Mrs. T., Margie and I have been though all the trials and tribulations of public elective office from eastern judge in the election of 1922, presiding judge in the election of 1926, U.S. Senator in 1934 and again in 1940. 1940 was a vicious personal smear affair. Then 1944 and 1948, both rough, tough affairs, as was 1952, a campaign for someone else.

There were rough times of service, locally, in the senate and as president of the United States, the greatest office in the history of the world—the greatest honor and the most awful responsibility to come to any man.

But that home town reception was worth all the effort, all the trials. Never has there been anything like it in Independence or any other ex-president's home town. I can never express to you adequately the appreciation of this family.

I've been taking my morning walks around the city and passing places that bring back wonderful recollections.

The Presbyterian Church at Lexington and Pleasant Streets where I started to Sunday School at the age of six years, where I first saw a lovely little golden-haired girl who is still the lovely lady—Margie's mother.

I pass by the Noland School where I first went to school in 1892. Had a white cap with [a] sign across...the cap's visor, which said Grover Cleveland for President and Adlai Stevenson for Vice President—the grandfather of the man I supported in 1952 sixty years later.

Just south of this building stood the old Columbian School, which was brand-new when I was ready for the third and fourth grades.

The Ott School over on Liberty and College where I was in the fifth grade under Aunt Nanny Wallace—Bess's aunt.

I pass the site of the old Independence High School at Maple and Pleasant. Ours was the first class to be graduated there, in 1901—fifty-two years ago.

And so it goes. What a pleasure to be back here at home—once more a free and independent citizen of the gateway city of the old Great West.

Our grandparents were citizens here in the county when the going was rough. They were real pioneers. They gave us our background of honor and integrity. I hope we've lived up to that heritage.

Thanks again, home folks, for a most happy return.[167]

Harry Truman focused on his presidential legacy, which included raising money to construct a library in his hometown. On July 7, 1954, Harry issued a press release that noted that he was pleased the officers and trustees of his presidential library had approved of locating the library in Independence. The release continued: "Independence has been my home for most of my life; it is where Mrs. Truman was born, where our daughter Margaret was born and where all of our close friends and family ties are. It is a great satisfaction to me to know that all the official papers of my entire public life will be housed in Independence."[168]

Harry Truman's February 5, 1953 homecoming speech. *Truman Library.*

On May 8, 1955, Harry Truman hosted a groundbreaking ceremony to signify the start of the construction of the Truman Library, and then afterward, guests attended a reception at 219 North Delaware. While the library was under construction, Harry utilized an office in the Federal Reserve Building in downtown Kansas City, and his presidential papers were housed temporarily at the Jackson County Courthouse in downtown Kansas City and later moved to the Memorial Building in Independence.[169]

While the construction of the Truman Library was important to him, he also furthered his legacy by writing about the presidency. In November 1955, Doubleday released the first volume, *Year of Decisions*, of his two-volume memoirs. The second volume, *Years of Trial and Hope*, was released the following year, in 1956. In 1960, Bernard Geis Associates released *Mr. Citizen* to the public, in which Harry Truman described what life was like as a private citizen in Independence. In 1961, the United States government printing office released the first volume of the *Public Papers of the Presidents*. The books were followed by a television series based on his memoirs titled *Decision: The Conflicts of Harry S. Truman*. A television crew taped twenty-

Harry Truman shovels dirt at the Truman Library groundbreaking ceremony, May 8, 1955. *Photograph by Harry Barth. Truman Library.*

six episodes that featured Truman discussing the most important decisions he made as president. The American Cinema Editors selected Truman as outstanding television personality for 1964.[170]

Life as a private citizen did not include Secret Service protection. The city of Independence provided the salary for Mike Westwood, who accompanied the former president on his walks and who also served as his driver. John Martino also served as a driver in the absence of Westwood. Rufus Burrus, the president's lifelong friend, who became the Truman family attorney, also frequently accompanied the president. In 1965, Congress authorized the protection of former presidents and their spouses, and in February 1966, the Secret Service established the Truman Protective Division and eventually managed the security detail by November 1970 from inside 224 North Delaware, just across the street from the Truman home.[171]

Life as a private citizen did not come with a pension either, until Congress approved one in August 1958. The legislation allocated former presidents $75,000 per year, and two-thirds of the appropriation was to be used for clerical assistance to help the president answer all of the letters that he received—only $25,000 went to Harry directly. The Trumans also had an investment portfolio that provided additional income, as did the proceeds from the sale of the Grandview farm.[172]

On April 21, 1956, Margaret Truman married Clifton Daniel—who at the time of the wedding was serving as an assistant to the foreign news editor of the *New York Times*—in the Trinity Episcopal Church in Independence. After the wedding, the couple lived in New York City, where she concentrated on a career in writing and publishing. In 1973, Clifton became chief of the *New York Times'* Washington Bureau. On June 5, 1957, the couple had the first of four children, Clifton Truman Daniel, followed by William Wallace Daniel, Harrison Gates Daniel and Thomas Washington Daniel.

While the Trumans were excited to assume the role of grandmother and grandfather, they were also elated about the dedication of the Truman

Left to right: Mr. Elbert Clifton Daniel, Mrs. Elvah Jones Daniel, Clifton Daniel, Margaret Truman, Mrs. Bess Wallace Truman and former president Harry S. Truman, by the staircase of the Truman home at 219 North Delaware, April 21, 1956. *Photograph by Sammie Feeback. Truman Library.*

Margaret Truman Daniel's sons as children, posing with baby Thomas Washington Daniel. *Left to right*: Harrison Gates Daniel, William Wallace Daniel and Clifton Truman Daniel (holding baby Thomas), circa 1966. *Truman Library.*

Library on July 6, 1957. Key guests included Eleanor Roosevelt, Speaker of the House Sam Rayburn, Senator Lyndon Johnson and Chief Justice Earl Warren, who delivered the keynote address. Mrs. Truman and members of her Bridge Club assisted with the reception, which the Trumans hosted for the distinguished guests at 219 North Delaware.[173]

Harry enjoyed spending time at the library, and according to John Curry, who worked at the library during this period, one of the most important activities Harry liked was meeting the schoolchildren who came to visit. Curry remembered, "No matter what he was doing in his office, someone might be working with him or visiting him…He would have them go into the auditorium, and he would go in and talk to them for a while. If he had someone who was visiting, he would take them along with him and introduce them to the school children."[174]

The community honored Harry Truman's seventy-fifth birthday on May 8, 1959, with a program in the RLDS Auditorium that was broadcast on closed-circuit TV to sixteen other cities. More than one thousand people

An aerial view of the Truman Library dedication, July 6, 1957. *Truman Library.*

turned out for the celebration in Independence, where family members and political associates recalled the relationships they had with the thirty-third president. One newspaper claimed that fifty thousand people joined in the celebration via the closed-circuit network.[175]

The Trumans settled into a routine, especially Harry, after the opening of the library. He described his routine in a September 1959 interview:

> *I usually get up about 5:00 or 5:30 A.M. and go downstairs and do a round of work going through the mail and the newspapers that come to me and along about 7:00 or 7:15 A.M., Mrs. Truman comes down and gets us a simple breakfast. We have breakfast and discuss things that take place during the day in the house and the yard and the people that are coming to work for us during the day and then about a quarter of eight, I get in the car and come over to the Library and sort out the mail...I work on it all the time and now I have help in the Library that takes dictation and files the letters and things of that sort and then along about 11:30 A.M., I go back over home and Mrs. Truman and I have lunch together. A very light lunch. Then I come back over to the library about 1:00 or 1:30 P.M. and finish up what I haven't been able to do in the morning and go back over home*

117

after I have signed all the mail and…take a nap, and then about 5:30 or 6:00 P.M. we begin to get ready for dinner which Mrs. Truman prepares. Then I go through a great many other documents…sometimes we look at television…and then about 9:30 or 10:00 o'clock, we go to bed.[176]

Harry also typically squeezed in a quick morning walk, "usually about six or six-thirty or seven o'clock," just before breakfast. His goal was 120 steps per minute, which he thought was necessary because "if you're going to take a walk for your physical benefit, it's necessary that you walk as if you're going someplace." He continued, "You swing your arms and take deep breaths."[177]

The Trumans hoped to spend more time with their friends and family; however, Harry was very busy in retirement. In September 1954, he wrote to cousin Ethel, "Things have come to a pretty pass when neighbors and relatives who live within a hundred yards of each other have to write letters to have a conversation." One year later, Harry's pace had not slowed when he told Ethel, "I think we are setting a record—next door neighbors, first cousins, and have to write when we talk."[178]

In May 1960, Natalie Wallace died following major surgery, and Frank passed away in August after a lengthy illness. Fred Wallace, Bess's younger brother, passed away in 1957, which left her with only one living brother, George; sadly, he died in May 1963. Vietta Garr remained with the family until she retired in the mid-1960s. The Trumans established a trust fund for her in 1957, and she died on December 31, 1973.[179]

Across the street, at 216 North Delaware, the Nolands aged as well. Nellie struggled with her health—challenges that began when Harry Truman was president. She died on August 8, 1958, leaving Ethel by herself in the home. Ethel continued to work on the Truman genealogy, and she remained active in the First Baptist Church, as well as the Mary Paxton Study Club, which studied classical literature, and the Browning Society. She died on August 10, 1971.[180]

Truman played an important role in the Democratic Party during his post-presidential years. John F. Kennedy came to Independence in November 1959 seeking Harry Truman's endorsement; however, Truman was concerned that John F. Kennedy was too young and did not immediately endorse his candidacy until later. After the voters elected Kennedy as president, he dispatched his vice president, Lyndon Baines Johnson, to travel to Independence to brief Truman on the Cuban Missile Crisis in April 1961; it was the first visit of many that LBJ would make to Independence as vice president and later as president.

Senator John F. Kennedy visits Harry Truman at the Truman Library, November 19, 1959. *Truman Library.*

Lyndon Johnson's most notable visit to Independence came on July 30, 1965, when he came to sign the landmark Medicare bill into law in the auditorium of the Truman Library. Johnson had returned to Independence because he credited Harry Truman with first proposing a greater role for the federal government to play in ensuring the health of all its citizens. Amid much fanfare, Truman told the crowd assembled, "I am glad to have lived this long and to witness today the signing of the Medicare bill which puts this Nation right where it needs to be, to be right." President Johnson then spoke and told the crowd:

> *It was a generation ago that Harry Truman said, and I quote him: "Millions of our citizens do not now have a full measure of opportunity to achieve and to enjoy good health. Millions do not now have protection or security against the economic effects of sickness. And the time has now arrived for action to help them attain that opportunity and to help them get the protection."*
>
> *Well today, Mr. President* [Truman], *and my fellow Americans, we are taking such action—20 years later.*[181]

Johnson returned to Independence on January 20, 1966, and gave Harry and Bess Truman Medicare cards "1" and "2."[182]

On October 11, 1968, Lyndon Johnson visited Harry Truman for the last time. Johnson came to 219 North Delaware, where he signed two presidential proclamations. The first proclamation discussed Truman's achievements as president, and the other proclaimed October 24 as United Nations Day because Truman signed the charter that established the UN.

The National Park Service recognized the importance that Independence played in Truman's life and political career when it approached the Truman family and asked them whether or not they would support the creation of a National Historic Landmark to honor the connections that Harry Truman had with his hometown. In September 1971, Harry wrote to his son-in-law, Clifton Daniel, who was working with the National Park Service on this issue and told him, "If it is the desire of those who have the authority to so designate the home and the area fronting on Delaware Street, as a National Historic Landmark we have no objections on such action." On November 11, 1971, the secretary of the interior created the Harry S Truman Historic District, National Historic Landmark (Truman NHL). Next to the establishment of the presidential library, the Truman NHL was the second most important designation that Independence could claim that commemorated the legacy of Harry Truman.[183]

On December 26, 1972, the former president passed away. In an elaborate funeral, which was planned several years in advance, Truman was laid to rest in the courtyard of his presidential library. John Haldeman, an Independence resident who first met Harry as a young boy at the age of eleven at the January 1953 homecoming, remembered that the lines

President Lyndon Johnson signs the Medicare bill into law in the auditorium of the Truman Library while Harry Truman looks on, July 30, 1965. *Truman Library.*

stretched all the way from the Truman Library past Highway 24 and on to Delaware Street. He got in the line at midnight, described the crowds as "huge" and recalled that it was a "very, very quiet, a[nd] dramatic scene." When he got inside the library, he remembered that marines

Harry S Truman Historic District National Historic Landmark

Independence, Missouri

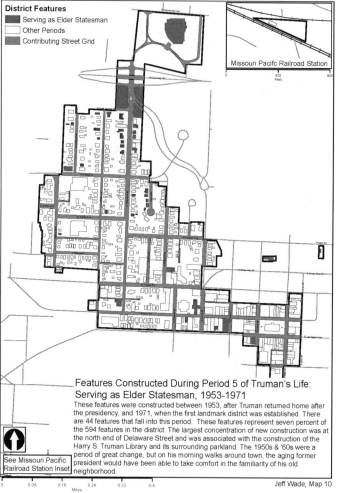

District Features
- ▓ Serving as Elder Statesman
- ☐ Other Periods
- ▓ Contributing Street Grid

Missouri Pacifc Railroad Station

Features Constructed During Period 5 of Truman's Life: Serving as Elder Statesman, 1953-1971

These features were constructed between 1953, after Truman returned home after the presidency, and 1971, when the first landmark district was established. There are 44 features that fall into this period. These features represent seven percent of the 594 features in the district. The largest concentration of new construction was at the north end of Delaware Street and was associated with the construction of the Harry S. Truman Library and its surrounding parkland. The 1950s & '60s were a period of great change, but on his morning walks around town, the aging former president would have been able to take comfort in the familiarity of his old neighborhood.

See Missouri Pacific Railroad Station Inset

Jeff Wade, Map 10

Map by Jeff Wade.

were standing at attention as he passed by the president's casket and that people would occasionally stop, but they were gently nudged forward in order to keep the line moving.[184]

Bess and her sister-in-law, May Wallace, were the last ones who remained at the Wallace family compound. Bess passed away at the age of ninety-seven on October 18, 1982. May Wallace died on May 18, 1993, at the age of ninety-eight. When Bess Truman passed away, the Truman family had already agreed that the home and most of its contents would be given to the people of the United States. On December 8, 1982, President Ronald Reagan signed an emergency proclamation that gave the National Park Service the authority to protect the home until Congress passed the enabling legislation to create the historic site. On May 23, 1983, Ronald Reagan signed the law that officially created the Harry S Truman National Historic Site. The creation of the national historic site marked the third nationally significant designation the city could claim that represented the life and legacy of the nation's thirty-third president. In 1989, Congress approved legislation to add the two Wallace homes on Truman Road and the Noland home on Delaware Street to the national park.

Conclusion

No man, no matter how great or how informed he may be, is capable of filling the Presidency of the United States in the manner in which it ought to be done. All any man can do is to do as best he can in the interests of all the people of the United States. He is a servant of all the people of the United States, and the United States is a servant of all the people in the world.

—Harry S. Truman[185]

H arry Truman spent sixty-four years of his life in Independence, Missouri. When he returned to Independence after serving as president, he wanted to produce a television series about the important decisions he made as president. A film crew descended on Independence to conduct interviews with the president and some of his closest associates. One of the crews filmed several outtakes at the Truman home, and in one clip, the film crew captured the former president coming out of 219 North Delaware, where he explained the importance of Independence:

> *Well it's good to be back home—in what I call the center of the world—Independence, Missouri. I think it's the greatest town in the United States. I have been all over the country. I have been to Europe, South America and several other places but I still like to come back home. I'll continue to feel that way as long as I live. I think you'll find everybody in Independence feels the same way about this town because it's the center of things for most of us and it's the center of things for*

me. I am more than happy to be here and to stay here the rest of my life. I hope I won't cause you too much trouble while I'm here.[186]

At the heart of Truman's center of the world was his neighborhood. That neighborhood included the schools he attended, where the teachers impressed on him the need to learn and he reciprocated by becoming a lifelong learner. As president, he wrote to his former teachers, and they wrote back. The community embraced the Latin inscription above the high school: *Juventus Spes Mundi* ("Youth Hope of the World"). That was a strong commitment the school made to its students before the Cold War, at a time in American history when the United States remained isolationist. Truman's administration presided over the United States exerting a greater role in world affairs, and he wanted to make sure that his neighbors in Independence, as well as all Americans, were aware of the new role the United States had to play. However, there was a challenge. What would govern the relationship between the United States and the rest of the world, especially those countries that had embraced Communism? Truman turned to his hometown for an answer, and he acknowledged it when he delivered the Liberty Bell dedication speech at the Memorial Building in 1950.

Moral codes and principles were important to him, and he found them in his Baptist faith but also in the Masonic teachings that he embraced. At his 1949 inauguration, it was not a coincidence that the two Bibles that he was sworn in on were opened to Exodus 20 (the Ten Commandments) and to Matthew 5 (the Sermon on the Mount). Harry Truman did not come across as an evangelical; however, he thought that the moral codes found in these passages were something that all people could support, and if they did, then this could help govern the relationship between the peoples of the world and their governments. He told his friend Rufus Burrus that "the meat of the whole thing [Sermon on the Mount] is that part of it which tells a man how to live with his neighbors, and instructs him that his welfare and benefit is wrapped up in that of his neighbors and his associates." Specifically, he thought that if his community of Independence abided by them, and if the United States and its allies abided by them, they would serve as an example as to how people and nations should treat one another in the Cold War.[187]

In May 1950, in a speech he delivered at the University of Wyoming in Laramie, he talked about how the distances between people and countries have shrunk and how "[w]e have become citizens of a larger

The First Presbyterian Church, where Harry Truman first met Bess Wallace but also where he learned that the American "concept of freedom has deep religious roots." *Truman Library.*

community—we are citizens of the world." He argued that at one time, the time when he was going to school in Independence, the United States would not pay attention to a country whose leadership exerted a significant amount of control over its people; however, he noted that this was a different time and that America's role in world affairs had changed:

We are next door neighbors now to people in other countries who once were scarcely more than names to us. We have become citizens of a larger community—we are citizens of the world.

It is the great problem—and the great challenge of our age—that strangers have become fellow citizens at a time when the world is so deeply divided. We have been forced into a common citizenship with peoples who do not understand our conception of democratic life. We must recognize—whether we like it or not—that we are neighbors with a government which denies all of the values of American tradition, indeed all the ethical and moral traditions, and which seeks to spread its doctrine over the entire earth. We have become neighbors of a new and terrible tyranny.

He continued to argue in the speech that it was increasingly difficult for democracy and tyranny to coexist because the world was much closer but also because the "new tyranny of Soviet communism is giving no evidence that it is willing to let the free world exist peacefully." He told the audience that the "free world must demonstrate moral superiority" that was based on scripture.[188] In a speech he delivered in June 1950 at the National Convention of the Augustana Lutheran Church, he told those assembled, "We have become the leaders of the moral forces of the world, the leaders who believe that the Sermon on the Mount means what it says, the leaders of that part of the world which believes that the law is the God-given law under which we live, that all our traditions have come from Moses at Sinai, and Jesus on the Mount."[189]

In a speech he delivered in Kansas City in December 1950, given when the United States was at war in Korea, he expanded on just exactly where Americans and the free world could derive their moral superiority that was needed to set an example in the Cold War:

It is a world situation. I have been trying to mobilize the moral forces of the world—Catholics, Protestants, Jews, the Eastern Church, the Grand Lama of Tibet, the Indian Sanskrit moral code—I have been trying to organize all those people to the understanding that their welfare and the existence of decency and honor in the world depends on our working together, and not trying to cut each other's throats.[190]

Harry Truman's view of the world was shaped by the moral code that was instilled in him by Independence's religious institutions and his membership in the Masons. The moral code did not mean that Independence was superior—it violated that code on two important occasions: first, when Independence leaders drove the Mormons from the town in the 1830s and again, in the 1960s, when poor whites and blacks were driven from an area of the city close to the Truman Library and the Independence Square, known as the "Neck" during urban renewal. However, to dismiss these instances as failures would belittle the complexities of how that code worked. It was part of Harry Truman's personal history, but he made it part of American and world history when he talked about how people and nations needed to act during the Cold War, and he connected his neighborhood with this larger narrative. Historians have yet to fully evaluate whether Harry Truman successfully persuaded Americans and other people or nations to use their moral code as a bulwark against the "evils" of Communism during the Cold War; however, his rhetoric was strong, and it originated from his experiences in Independence.[191]

During the presidency, Harry's community did seem to understand the new role the United States would play in world affairs and that their role was to be a source of strength and encouragement to the president and first family while they were in office. Frank Rucker, editor of the *Independence Examiner* in 1946, evaluated Independence's "First Year in the White House":

First of all, we have been brought to know that we no longer belong to ourselves alone, but that our town belongs to the people just as the President belongs to them. We have, we believe, met that situation with the same free and easy manner that the President has met it...We have extended our hospitality to visitors and sightseers in the best manner we know how, and have enjoyed it...

Just as naturally as being President has broadened the vision and understanding of Mr. Truman, so has being the President's home town widened our vision and increased our understanding of the problems that confront a nation in this period of world reconstruction. We have read every word that the President has said on matters of state and of world policy... Through all this we have grown in wisdom and stature as citizens.

Harry Truman responded to the editorial and thanked Rucker for writing it: "It confirms what I know already; namely, that Independence has borne up well under the strain. I knew it would. If history records that I have done half so well as my fellow townsmen, I shall be satisfied."[192]

Today, Independence has become the keeper of Harry Truman's historical legacy. It is found in the Harry S. Truman Library and Museum, the Harry S

Harry Truman preparing to take a stroll through his neighborhood, November 18, 1954. *Photograph by Sammie Feeback. Truman Library.*

Truman National Historic Site and along the streets, landscapes and buildings found in the Harry S Truman Historic District, National Historic Landmark. However, it is not just Truman's history; the city of Independence influenced Harry Truman, and he in turn influenced his hometown. As one resident of the city noted in 1979, "I think that every person that grew up in Independence in the time period or older, as my parents, feel a personal relationship with Harry Truman. And they feel that they have something special that nobody else has. But I think it's pretty universal...And they're always proud when somebody says, 'Where are you from?' It's always, 'Harry Truman's town, Independence.'"[193]

Notes

The Gates/Wallace and Truman Families Come to Independence, 1865-1902

1. Harry S. Truman, *Public Papers of the Presidents, 1952* (Washington, D.C.: USGPO, 1966), 748–49.
2. See William Patrick O'Brien, "Independence, Missouri's Trade with Mexico, 1827–1860: A Study in International Consensus and Cooperation" (PhD diss., University of Colorado, 1994).
3. George W. Gates to George P. Gates, September 27, 1865, in 1865 folder, Correspondence File, George Porterfield Gates Papers (hereafter GPGP), Harry S. Truman Library (hereafter HSTL), Independence, Missouri. For George W. Gates's purchase of property in Independence, see George W. Gates to George P. Gates, March 2, 1866, and March 5, 1866, in 1866 folder, GPGP, HSTL.
4. For the birthdates of Madge, Maud and Myra, see Ron Cockrell, *The Trumans of Independence: Historic Resource Study* (Omaha, NE: Midwest Region of the National Park Service, 1985), 20. For George P. Gates's arrival in Independence, see Edward Payson Gates to George P. Gates, November 22, 1866, in 1866 folder, Correspondence File, GPGP, HSTL.
5. For the Hannibal Bridge, see Cockrell, *Trumans of Independence*, 23.
6. For the partnership between George P. Gates and William H. Waggoner, see Waggoner & Gates folder, GPGP, HSTL.
7. See information in Printed Materials folder, GPGP, HSTL.
8. Cockrell, *Trumans of Independence*, 24–26.
9. Henry C. Chiles, interview by J.R. Fuchs, November 1, 1961, transcript, 19, HSTL.
10. Ibid., 44–45. Also, Cockrell noted that the *Directory of Independence for 1889–90* listed the David W. Wallace family as residing at 219 North Delaware.
11. Mary Paxton Keeley, interview by J.R. Fuchs, June 11, 1976, transcript, 22–23, HSTL.
12. Ibid., 50.

13. Ibid., 24, 28.

14. Ibid., 30.

15. Ibid., 44–45.

16. Gail E.H. Evans and Michael Hatch, National Register of Historic Places Registration Form, 606 to 605, Truman Road, Section 8, page 21.

17. *Official Manual of the State of Missouri, 1911–1912* (Jefferson City, MO: Hugh Stephens Printing Company), 673.

18. Mary Ethel Noland, interview by J.R. Fuchs, August 23, 1965, transcript, 40–42, HSTL.

19. Jon E. Taylor, *Truman's Grandview Farm* (Charleston, SC: The History Press, 2011), 11–14.

20. For the quote, see Harry S. Truman, *Year of Decisions*, vol. 1 (Garden City, NY: Doubleday & Company, 1955), 115.

21. Mary Ethel Noland, interview by J.R. Fuchs, September 9, 1965, transcript, 81, HSTL.

22. Truman, *Memoirs*, I, 116.

23. Chiles interview, 10–11.

24. Truman, *Memoirs*, I, 117.

25. Chiles interview, 5–6.

26. Chiles interview, 5, 9.

27. Raymond Geselbracht, "A Boy Who Would Be President: Harry Truman at School, 1892–1901," Prologue 36, no. 3 (Fall 2004).

28. Raymond Geselbracht, *Truman Places*, brochure, 1995.

29. Mize Peters, interview by J.R. Fuchs, August 8, 1963, transcript, 1, HSTL.

30. Truman, *Memoirs*, I, 116–19.

31. Gail E.H. Evans and Michael Hatch, National Register of Historic Places Registration Form, 216 North Delaware, Section 8, page 3.

32. Noland interview, 70–71.

HABERDASHER AND COUNTY JUDGE, 1919–1933

33. Harry S. Truman (hereafter HST) to Bess Truman, April 15, 1933, Papers Pertaining to Family Business and Personal Affairs (hereafter PPFBPA), HSTL.

34. Keeley interview, 41.

35. For more on these pursuits and Truman's early Masonic career, see Taylor, *Truman's Grandview Farm*, 56–70.

36. Ibid., 81. Also see Robert H. Ferrell, ed., *Dear Bess* (New York: W.W. Norton & Company, 1983).

37. Gail E.H. Evans and Michael Hatch, National Register of Historic Places Registration Form, 601 and 605 Truman Road, Section 8, page 24.

38. *Independence Examiner*, September 15, 1917, 4.

39. Mary Ann Sturges to Bess Wallace, September 17, 1917, in Folder "S," Box 33, Papers of Bess Wallace Truman (hereafter PBWT), HSTL.

40. Evans and Hatch, National Register Form, 601 and 605 Truman Road, Section 8, page 23.

41. HST, in 1919 folder, Vertical File, HSTL.

42. Adelaide Twyman to Bess Wallace, undated, in Folder "T," Box 33, PBWT, HSTL.

43. For information on the construction of the homes, see Evans and Hatch, National Register Form, 601 and 605 Truman Road, Section 8, page 27. For Natalie's letter, see the PBWT, HSTL.

44. HST to C.Z. Coffin, September 21, 1921, in American Legion Convention folder, September 1921, PPFBPA, HSTL.

45. Alonzo Hamby, *Man of the People: A Life of Harry S. Truman* (New York: Oxford University Press, 1995), 91–92.

46. HST to Ernest Schmidt, February 4, 1922, in Correspondence General, January–July 1922 folder, PPFBPA, HSTL.

47. Robert H. Ferrell, *Harry S. Truman: A Life* (Columbia: University of Missouri Press, 1994), 96.

48. Rufus Burrus, interview by Niel M. Johnson, October 22, 1985, transcript, 18–21, HSTL.

49. Ferrell, *Harry S. Truman*, 95–96.

50. Affidavit challenging the August 1, 1922 primary, August 9, 1922, in Correspondence General, 1921 folder, PPFBPA, HSTL.

51. Campaign expenses, August 19, 1922, in Correspondence General, August–September 1922 folder, PPFBPA, HSTL.

52. HST to W.C. Duvall, August 14, 1922, in Correspondence General, January–July 1922 folder, PPFBPA, HSTL.

53. Campaign advertisement, Jackson County Court Election folder, 1922, PPFBPA, HSTL.

54. See www.whitehouse.gov/about/presidents/warrenharding.

55. L.A. Lohman to HST, October 14, 1922, in Correspondence General, October–December 1922 folder, PPFBPA, HSTL.

56. Undated campaign contribution list, in Correspondence General, October–December 1922 folder, PPFBPA, HSTL.

57. Harry Abbot, interview by Niel M. Johnson, April 4, 1990, transcript, 11–13, HSTL.

58. For the letters, see HST to Fourteenth Precinct Democratic Club and HST to W.A. Hill, both letters dated February 3, 1923, in Correspondence General, 1923 folder, PPFBPA, HSTL.

59. For the election results, see Hamby, *Harry S. Truman*, 126.

60. Ibid., 130.

61. Chiles interview, 47–48.

62. Hamby, *Man of the People*, 130.

63. Ibid., 90–92.

64. Bess to HST, [July 26, 1923], reprinted in Clifton Truman Daniel, *Dear Harry Love Bess: Bess Truman's Letters to Harry Truman, 1919–1943* (Kirksville, MO: Truman State University Press, 2011), 30.

65. Ibid., 36.

66. Ibid.

67. Ibid., 39.

68. See Richard Lawrence Miller, *Truman: The Rise to Power* (New York: McGraw Hill), 205–16.

69. See Jon E. Taylor, *A President, a Church, and Trails West: Competing Histories in Independence, Missouri* (Columbia: University of Missouri Press, 2008), 55–58.

70. Miller, *Truman*, 217–19.

71. Jennie Johnson, interview by Niel M. Johnson, July 25, 1989, transcript, 14–15, 52, HSTL.

72. Mrs. W.L.C. Palmer, interview by J.R. Fuchs, January 18, 1962, transcript, 32–33, HSTL.

73. Miller, *Truman*, 220.

74. See Hamby, *Man of the People*, for the "overriding objective," 149; for Stayton's role in 1924, 122; and for the number of miles of road and cost, 151.

75. Ibid., 151.

76. Ferrell, *Harry S. Truman*, 111–12.

77. Ibid.

78. Ibid.

79. For the pageant, see *Independence Examiner*, "A Pageant and a Horseshow Too," September 7, 1933. For the attendance figure, see *Independence Examiner*, September 8, 1933.

80. Ferrell, *Harry S. Truman*, 113.

81. Hamby, *Man of the People*, 184.

82. Ibid., 184–85. For the resignation date, see Miscellaneous Historical Documents Collection (hereafter MHDC), 820, HSTL.

83. *Independence Examiner*, August 7, 1934.

84. Ibid., August 6, 1934.

85. Ibid., "Truman Power Irresistible," August 8, 1934.

86. Ibid., "The Nomination of Judge Truman," August 8, 1934.

87. Ibid., "Truman First Senator from Independence," November 7, 1934.

88. Ibid., "Independence Home of Senator," November 7, 1934.

89. *Kansas City Star*, "Regret with Her Thrills," November 7, 1934, 1–2.

U.S. SENATOR AND VICE PRESIDENT, 1934-1945

90. Mrs. W.L.C. Palmer, interview by J.R. Fuchs, January 18, 1962, transcript, 32–33, HSTL.

91. Mr. and Mrs. Olney Burrus to Truman family, July 23, 1944, Folder "B," Box 34, PBWT, HSTL.

92. *Independence Examiner*, "Independence in Farewell Toast to the Trumans," December 18, 1934.

93. Ibid., December 28, 1934.

94. Barbara Allen Gard interview, by Jim Williams, August 27, 1991, transcript, 18, Harry S Truman NHS.

95. E-mail correspondence with Randy Sowell, January 24, 2013.

96. *Independence Examiner*, January 4, 1935.

97. HST to Bess, June 28, 1935, PPFBPA, HSTL.

98. Madge to Bess, [March 20, 1936], January–March 1936 folder; [April 3, 1936, and April 11, 1936 letters], April 1936 folder, PBWT, HSTL.

99. Ibid., June 28 [1936], PPFBPA, HSTL.

100. Ibid., January 26, 1937, PPFBPA, HSTL.

101. Hamby, *Man of the People*, 218–21.

102. For more on the political situation, see Ferrell, *Harry S. Truman*, 144–45. For the illness, see HST to Bess, September 15 [1937], PPFBPA, HSTL.

103. For the doctor's recommendation of more physical exercise, see Hamby, *Man of the People*, 211–12. For the morning walks starting as a U.S. senator, see Harry Truman, *Mr. Citizen* (New York: Bernard Geis Associates), 31. In a letter Harry sent to Bess on December 7, 1937, he told her that he used the cold morning as an excuse to "miss my walk." In a subsequent letter, he told her, "I walked about two miles this morning." See HST to Bess, December 13, 1937, PPFBPA, HSTL.

104. HST to Bess, November 7, 1937, PPFBPA, HSTL.

105. HST to Bess, December 5, 1937, PPFBPA, HSTL.

106. Hamby, *Man of the People*, 224–25.

107. Ibid., 230.

108. Lawrence H. Larsen and Nancy J. Hulston, *Pendergast!* (Columbia: University of Missouri Press, 1997), 144–64.

109. For this paragraph, see Ferrell, *Dear Bess*, 419–37. For the December letter, see HST to Bess, December 15, 1939, PPFBPA, HSTL.

110. Ferrell, *Harry S. Truman*, 148–49.

111. For more on the 1940 Senate campaign, see Robert H. Ferrell, *Truman and Pendergast* (Columbia: University of Missouri Press, 1999).

112. Ferrell, *Harry S. Truman*, 152.

113. HST to Bess, August 9, 1940, PPFBPA, HSTL.

114. For the election results, see Hamby, *Harry S. Truman*, 247.

115. See Hamby, *Man of the People*, 248–51, and Ferrell, *Harry S. Truman*, 155–59.

116. HST to Bess, December 7, 1941, PPFBPA, HSTL.

117. Madge to Bess, [July 22, 1944], Madge to Bess July–September 1944 folder, PBWT, HSTL.

118. Natalie Wallace to Bess Truman, Natalie Ott Wallace 1933–1951 folder, PBWT, HSTL.

119. See *Kansas City Star*, July 23, 1944; Margaret Truman, *Souvenir* (New York: McGraw-Hill), 68; Cockrell, *Trumans of Independence*, 143. For Mrs. D.W. Wallace in Denver, Colorado, see Madge to Bess [July 20, 1944], Madge to Bess July–September 1944 folder, PBWT, HSTL.

120. HST to Bess, August 18, 1944, PPFBPA, HSTL.

121. Cockrell, *Trumans of Independence*, 146.

122. Natalie Wallace to Bess Truman, [January 29, 1945], Natalie Ott Wallace 1933–1951 folder, PBWT, HSTL.

PRESIDENT AND FIRST LADY, 1945-1953

123. L.L. Compton to Mrs. Truman, April 12, 1951, Folder "C" (2 of 2), PBWT, HSTL.

124. For the letter, see HST to May Wallace, April 12, 1945, Correspondence with Harry S Truman folder, Papers of Mary "May" Wallace, HSTL. For a more detailed account of how Truman became president, see Ferrell, *Harry S. Truman*, 176-78.

125. Ferrell, *Harry S. Truman*, 176-78.

126. Natalie Wallace to Bess Wallace, [undated, but after April 12, 1945], undated Natalie Ott Wallace folder, PBWT, HSTL.

127. *Kansas City Times*, "Home Town Calm," April 13, 1945.

128. For the statement about the fence, see Nellie Noland to HST, December 16, 1950; for the lights burning, see Nellie Noland to HST, December 16, 1950, Mary Ethel and Nellie Noland 1950 folder, PBWT, HSTL.

129. *Kansas City Times*, "Home Town Calm," April 13, 1945.

130. George S. Dodsworth to HST, April 13, 1945, President's Personal File (hereafter PPF) 125, HSTL.

131. Ibid.

132. Henry Bundschu to HST, April 21, 1945, and May 3, 1945, PPF 868, HSTL.

133. "Rains Delay Rush Paint Job on Truman's Independence Home," June 1945, Vertical File, HSTL.

134. *Independence Examiner*, June 4, 1945.

135. The four paragraphs about Vietta are based on the National Park Service brochure *Vietta Garr*, published in 2004.

136. Barbara Allen Gard, interview by James H. Williams, August 27, 1991, transcript, 53-54, Harry S Truman NHS.

137. *Kansas City Star*, "Harry's on His Way Home to Just Rest and Visit a Bit," June 15, 1945.

138. Ibid.

139. *Kansas City Star*, "Spruce Up for Truman," June 15, 1945.

140. The preceding paragraphs were based on newspaper clippings in the HSTL Vertical File.

141. Truman, *Public Papers of the Presidents, 1945*, 144-47.

142. *Independence Examiner*, June 28, 1945.

143. *Independence Examiner*, "President Truman Off to a Smiling Start at 9 a.m," June 28, 1945.

144. *Kansas City Times*, "Back to the Capitol," September 17, 1945.

145. *Independence Examiner*, December 20, 1945.

146. See Ernest Capps to HST, December 14, 1945, and HST to Capps, December 15, 1945, PPF 2296, HSTL; Mize Peters to HST, December 18, 1945, and HST to Peters, December 21, 1945, PPF 623, HSTL.

147. Truman, *Public Papers of the Presidents, 1948*, 967-68.

148. *Kansas City Times*, "Truman Is Home," November 1, 1948.

149. *Independence Examiner*, November 1, 1948.

150. Truman, *Public Papers of the Presidents, 1948*, 939.

151. Hamby, *Man of the People*, 463.

152. Truman, *Public Papers of the Presidents, 1948*, 940-41.

153. HST to Ray Wills, May 26, 1948, and Wills to HST, November 14, 1948, PPF 3193, HSTL; Luke Choplin to HST, November 3, 1948, and HST to Choplin, November 22, 1948, PPF 4374, HSTL.

154. John and Edna Hutchison to HST, November 3, 1948, and HST to the Hutchisons, November 15, 1948, PPF 2985, HSTL.

155. *Independence Examiner*, December 27 and 29, 1948.

156. *Independence Examiner*, January 17 and 24, 1949.

157. HST to Mr. Frank Brown, February 6, 1950, PPF 469, HSTL.

158. "Speech as Delivered," November 6, 1950, Box 904, Official File 200-3-S, HSTL.

159. Ardelia Hardin Palmer to HST, November 9, 1950, PPF 1127, HSTL.

160. Nellie Noland to HST, October 29, 1951, Mary Ethel and Nellie Noland folder, 1951, PBWT, HSTL.

161. Mary Ethel Noland to HST, February 23, 1952, Mary Ethel and Nellie Noland 1952 folder, PBWT, HSTL.

162. George H. Gallup, *The Gallup Poll: Public Opinion, 1935–1971*, vol. 2, *1949–1958* (New York: Random House, 1972), 1,114.

163. *Decision: The Conflicts of Harry S. Truman*, Columbia Pictures, 1964, transcript, HSTL.

RETURNING TO INDEPENDENCE, 1953-1982

164. Truman, *Mr. Citizen*, 86.

165. *Decision*, transcript, HSTL.

166. Blevins Davis to Robert Weatherford, January 28, 1953, and February 5, 1953, Testimonial Dinner folder, Post Presidential Papers (hereafter PPP), Box 724.

167. "February 5, 1953" folder, Longhand notes, President's Secretary's File (hereafter PSF), Box 284, HSTL.

168. Press release, July 7, 1954, MHDC 109, HSTL.

169. James R. Fuchs, interview by Monte Poen, June 20, 1979, transcript, 1, Papers of Monte Poen, HSTL.

170. See Truman Library website, http://trumanlibrary.org/decision/videos.htm.

171. Cockrell, *Trumans of Independence*, 342.

172. Ibid., 329.

173. *Independence Examiner*, "Reception at Home to Follow Dedication," July 5, 1957.

174. John T. Curry, interview by Monte Poen, November 18, 1980, transcript, 22–23, John T. Curry folder, Papers of Monte Poen, HSTL.

175. *Kansas City Star*, May 8, 1959; *St. Louis Post-Dispatch*, May 8, 1959; *Kansas City Times*, May 9, 1959; *Independence Examiner*, May 9, 1959.

176. Interviews with President Truman conducted by David Noyes and William Hillman, 1959, Tape No. 9, October 21, 1959, folder 1, PPP, HSTL.

177. Thursday afternoon conference, p. 26, September 10, 1959, folder 1, PPP, HSTL.

178. Gail E.H. Evans-Hatch and D. Michael Evans-Hatch, *Farm Roots and Family Ties: Historic Resource Study, the Harry S Truman Grandview Farm, the Wallace houses, and the Noland House in Independence* (Silverton, OR: Evans-Hatch & Associates, 2001), 195.

179. *Vietta Garr* brochure.

180. Evans-Hatch and Evans-Hatch, *Farm Roots and Family Ties*, 199.

181. Lyndon B. Johnson, *Public Papers of the Presidents, 1965*, Book 2 (Washington, D.C.: USGPO, 1966), 812–14. For more on Truman's role in healthcare, see Monte Poen, *Harry S. Truman Versus the Medical Lobby* (Columbia: University of Missouri Press, 1979).

182. Lyndon B. Johnson, *Public Papers of the Presidents, 1966*, Book 1 (Washington, D.C.: USGPO, 1967), 44.

183. HST to Clifton Daniel, September 3, 1971, Historic Preservation Data 1968–72, folder 1, IHC File, Zobrist Papers, HSTL.

184. John Haldeman, interview by Monte Poen, July 26, 1979, transcript, 11, Papers of Monte Poen, HSTL.

CONCLUSION

185. Truman, *Public Papers of the Presidents, 1950*, 463.

186. *Decision*, transcript, HSTL.

187. HST to Rufus Burrus, October 18, 1949, PPF 736, HSTL.

188. Truman, *Public Papers of the Presidents, 1950*, 333–38.

189. Ibid., 463.

190. Ibid., 757.

191. For more on the Mormon removal, see Stephen C. LeSuer, *The 1838 Mormon War in Missouri* (Columbia: University of Missouri Press, 1987); for urban renewal, see Taylor, *A President, a Church, and Trails West*, 101–10. For historians who have thought about Truman's religious influences, see Elizabeth Edwards Spalding, *The First Cold Warrior: Harry Truman, Containment, and the Remaking of Liberal Internationalism* (Lexington: University Press of Kentucky, 2006), 205–22, and Richard S. Kirkendall, "Faith and Foreign Policy: An Exploration into the Mind of Harry Truman," *Missouri Historical Review* 102, no. 4 (July 2008): 214–25.

192. *Independence Examiner*, April 12, 1946; HST to Frank Rucker, April 16, 1946, PPF 433, HSTL.

193. John Haldeman, interview by Monte Poen, July 26, 1979, transcript, 5, John Haldeman folder, Papers of Monte Poen, HSTL.

Index

About the Author

J on Taylor is a former historian at Harry S Truman National Historic Site and associate professor of history at the University of Central Missouri in Warrensburg, Missouri. He holds a PhD in history from the University of Missouri–Columbia. He is also author of *Truman's Grandview Farm* (also available from The History Press), *Freedom to Serve: Truman, Civil Rights, and EO 9981* and *A President, a Church, and Trails West: Competing Histories in Independence, Missouri.*